D0712556

HOW TO ◆
PLAN &
DEVELOP
A CAREER
CENTER

SECOND EDITION

DONALD A. SCHUTT JR.
GENERAL EDITOR

Ferguson Publishing
An imprint of Infobase Publishing

How to Plan and Develop a Career Center, Second Edition

Copyright © 2008 by Infobase Publishing

Ferguson
An imprint of Infobase Publishing
132 West 31st Street
New York, NY 10001

Library of Congress Cataloging-in-Publication Data

Schutt, Donald A.
   How to plan and develop a career center / Don Schutt. — 2nd ed.
   p. cm.
   Includes bibliographical references and index.
   ISBN-13: 978-0-8160-7135-7
   ISBN-10: 0-8160-7135-7
   1. Career education—Information services—United States—Planning.
   2. Vocational guidance—Information services—United States—Planning.
   I. J.G. Ferguson Publishing Company. II. Title.
   LC1037.5.S38 2007
   370.11'30973—dc22
                                  2007010704

Text design by Annie O'Donnell
Cover design by Takeshi Takahashi

Printed in the United States of America

MP FOF 10 9 8 7 6 5 4 3 2 1

This book is printed on acid-free paper.

CONTENTS

ACKNOWLEDGEMENTS

It seems like there have been many significant changes in the world since the first edition of this book. It would have been difficult to imagine in 1999 that which unfolded on September 11, 2001, or the devastation that occurred in New Orleans, the war in Iraq, or more recently the tragic shootings at Virginia Tech. The impact of these and other events have created a ripple effect on individuals and their hopes, dreams, and plans. Career development, the intersection where individuals connect with the world of work, has also responded to these changes. This second edition reflects those changes in an effort to keep pace with an ever-changing society.

The editor would like to thank the authors of both editions for their generosity in sharing their time, expertise, and experience. In this edition Judith Ettinger, Pat Fessenden, Jane Finkle, Jane Goodman, Brian M. Montalvo, Ken Patch, Sybil Pressprich, Becky Ryan, Pat Schwallie-Giddis, and George Watson responded to the call for assistance in bringing this book into the new century. Their responsiveness and hard work created timely and useful chapters that extend the application of the first edition. The editor would also like to thank the contributing authors of the first edition.

In addition, the editor would like to thank James Chambers at Ferguson Publishing for his support, problem solving, and patience throughout the process, as well as the staff at Ferguson Publishing for their feedback, precision, and attention to detail. Thanks also to Roger Lambert, formerly at the Center on Education and Work at the University of Wisconsin-Madison, for his vision and entrepreneurial skills that brought the first edition to market. Special thanks to John Allen, whose technical expertise and timing will not be forgotten. Lastly, the editor thanks his family for understanding and supporting his passion for career development.

INTRODUCTION

by Donald A. Schutt Jr.

Not so long ago, career centers focused almost exclusively on matching people to jobs—the so-called trait and factor approach. Clients' aptitudes and abilities were assessed, generally at the high school level, the results of those assessments then being used to inform clients of the "right" job or the "right" postsecondary education for them. Direct placement services were sometimes offered but, as often as not, clients were left to find employment through family contacts or the classified ads.

Within this narrow range of goals, these old career centers frequently met with success. As the world of work began to change, however, career centers based on the trait and factor approach became less able to serve their clients effectively. At the same time, educational and training opportunities were expanding: access to universities increased for women, racial and ethnic minorities, and the less affluent; vocational courses at technical schools opened doors for those previously shut out of the old apprenticeship and on-the-job training systems. Career centers still operating on the notion that one person in one job equals a career could hardly hope for success in such a world.

Yet further changes await even those centers that tried to adapt to the broadened definition of *career* as a lifetime of growth and achievement instead of a solitary job and to accept the expanded horizons of every person inhabiting the world of work. Today's workplace must address the new concerns of diversity, downsizing, lifelong learning, and the astonishing progress of technology. Whether they serve second graders or senior citizens, assembly line workers or academic researchers, career centers must take all of these factors into account and provide services geared toward today's world of work—and ready for tomorrow's.

More specifically, career centers play a vital role in preparing youth, transitioning adults, and assisting new workers be both prepared and able to access information and services. America's Career Resource Network (ACRN) summarized the current situation: "Work and workplaces are changing in response to technological innovation and global competition. Employers need more workers with high-level skills. However, the U.S. workforce is aging, and the number of young skilled workers is not increasing. This points to a significant labor and skills shortage if steps are not taken now to counter this trend" (ACRN, retrieved from http://www.acrnetwork.org/econchal.htm on November 12, 2006).

Further, they reported:

- The number of people 55 and over will increase sharply by 2050, but their labor force participation will increase only slightly. This means the overall labor force will shrink.
- By 2010, there will be a shortage of nearly 8 million workers. The United States will need to import skilled workers from abroad.
- Already, immigrants are responsible for a large share of labor force growth (they account for almost half of the growth between 1996–2000).
- A National Association of Manufacturers' survey found that 80 percent of responding businesses said they had a "moderate to serious" shortage of qualified job candidates.
- There are currently 44.2 million people in the 36–45 age group, compared to 39.4 million people in the 26–46 age group. Over the next 30 years, the percentage of Americans age 65 or older will increase to more than 20 percent as the U.S. baby boom generation turns 65.
- By 2010, more than 42 percent of all jobs in the economy will require a vocational certificate, associate's degree, bachelor's degree, or higher.
- 65 percent of the fastest growing occupations in the US require some form of postsecondary education (associate's degree, vocational certificate, bachelor's degree).

- Of the 30 fastest growing occupations, 21(or 70 percent) generally require a postsecondary degree or other training beyond high school.
- By 2014, the workforce will have openings for 9 million more degree holders than will be available. There will be 3 million surplus openings for two-year degree holders, 4 million for four-year degree holders, and 2 million for advanced degree holders.
- Increasingly, U.S. employers are turning to foreign nationals for skilled work. In 2003, nearly 15 percent of employees in the U.S. workforce were foreign born.
- Almost half of this nation's current adult population reads at levels 1 and 2, which is below the literacy level expected of the average high school graduate.
- The U.S. population is getting more diverse. By 2050, there will be no majority race, and the young workforce will be increasingly minority.
- The labor force, therefore, will be increasingly made up of racial minorities who do not have the educational qualifications to obtain and succeed in the highly skilled jobs of the future. African Americans and Hispanics could fall increasingly behind economically. (Condensed from ACRN, retrieved from http://www.acrnetwork.org/econchal.htm on November 12, 2006).

These trends provide direction for career centers including: a renewed sense of importance regarding youth and their career decisions, an increased focus on providing services to adults in transition, an increased level of sophistication of use of the Internet in career development, and attention to the needs of increased numbers of workers coming from outside of the United States for employment.

Many of you might think this is easier said than done, but as with most challenging problems, things become less complicated when the main task of career centers is broken down into its components. According to the National Career Development Association (NCDA), career centers can meet the needs of both adults and youth in the community by providing:

- extensive self-appraisal, using a wide variety of instruments related to lifelong career development;
- extensive career information, including local, state, and national data concerning a wide variety of occupations as well as the education/training needed for each;
- career counseling services conducted by qualified professionals;
- career training facilities designed to help persons acquire necessary skills for finding and keeping a job, making career decisions, and identifying personal work values; and
- career placement and follow-up services.

(Adapted from Engels 1994)

In many ways, the key to effectiveness is not in offering each of the NCDA's five suggested services in isolation, but in offering all of them as part of a process. While Wessel (1998) discussed this need in college-level career centers, the thoughts easily translate to all centers: "We must be able to help students not only identify skills and interests, but to also inform students how those skills and interests are used in a work setting. We must maintain an active network of employer and alumni contacts in order to keep current." When the modern career center gives its clients the tools to succeed, when it teaches and assists in career development instead of job placement, it fulfills the mandate it has received from the modern world of work.

This book is designed, quite simply, to help today's career centers fulfill that mandate. Whether you are planning and developing a career center from scratch or overhauling an existing entity, blessed with resources or operating under appreciable constraints, serving a small and specific population or a large and varied one, this book can help. Two new chapters have been added to this edition: Chapter 10: Corporate Career Centers was added to address the growing number of employers paying closer attention the to changing workforce conditions identified earlier; Chapter 11: Partnering with Employers to Offer Career Development and Planning Services discusses the entrepreneurial opportunities for career centers to work with employers to provide both on-site and off-site services as a way for career centers to generate revenue. In addition, Chapter 8: Adult Career Centers: An Overview has been rewritten to offer updated research to the adjustment and readjustment processes many adults now bring to career centers; Chapter 9: One-Stop Career Centers for Adults expands on the topic and provides insights into the application of the ideas to the center. The influence of the Internet has also been integrated into the chapters, particularly Chapter 12: Career Centers on the Internet. Also integrated into select chapters is the impact on career centers of working with users who speak multiple languages. This new edition still follows a simple, four-stage process: planning, developing, implementing, and improving. Integrated within the process are such topics as marketing, access, and technology, so that they are not viewed in isolation.

The *planning* stage involves formulating both a philosophical foundation and concrete strategy for producing the functioning physical entity. Chapters 1 and 2 take you through this stage by providing more information on the role of today's career centers and raising the questions and concerns that each center must address.

The second stage, *developing*, works out the practical aspects of creating (or re-creating, as the case may be) a career center. Chapters 3 through 5 seek to turn your plans for the physical center into reality by addressing issues of space and furnishings, materials, and management of the facility.

A well-furnished, efficiently run center is no success unless it effectively connects to its target clientele—and that is the aim of the third stage, *implementing*. Chapters 6 through 12 address the needs of career centers serving different populations in various environments.

The final stage of planning and developing a career center is *improving* it. Chapter 13 provides an action plan that concludes with an assessment of the center's room for improvement. Lest you think that the developmental work on your career center is at an end, you will find that there really is always room for improvement—and that the way to improve your center is to return to stage one.

Chapter 14 addresses concerns facing career centers in the very near future and additional changes that are already beginning to affect the world of work. These items should be in the back of your mind as you work through each stage of constructing your career center.

Rather than feel intimidated or threatened by the changes and indeed the pace of change in the modern world of work, career center personnel can confidently undertake their important and challenging mission of helping individuals to create their own fulfilling and dynamic careers.

SUMMARY

Over the past three decades, career centers have shifted their focus from matching people with jobs to facilitating lifelong career planning and learning. Effective career centers provide means of self-appraisal, career information, career counseling services, career training facilities, and career placement and follow-up services. To reach this level of comprehensiveness, career centers must set in motion a cyclical process of planning, developing, implementing, and improving.

CHAPTER 1

Career Development and the Role of Career Centers

by Donald A. Schutt Jr.

I t is the role of the modern career center to support and empower individuals to create and use personally meaningful career plans. Career centers can help individuals become "more self-directed and proactive in their own promotions and advancements, to make their needs known, [and] to empower themselves" (Hansen 1997). To better understand the career development process and the role of career centers, it is important first to define the conceptual components.

CONCEPTUAL COMPONENTS

The following concepts provide the foundation on which effective career centers operate. Identifying the meanings of concepts early in the process and creating a shared set of definitions can decrease miscommunication and misdirection as the program grows. The terms career, career development, career guidance, and career counseling all have had variable meanings over the past two decades, the latter two terms generally changing to reflect the other two. As Hansen (1997) noted that "both anecdotal sources and formal surveys reveal that the public still views 'career' primarily as 'job' and that the outcome of vocational planning is often choosing a job," these clarifications are necessary to provide an effective delivery of services and also to educate career center users.

1

Career has been defined as a "life style concept that involves a sequence of work or leisure activities in which one engages throughout a lifetime. A career is unique to each person and is dynamic and unfolding throughout life. Careers include not only occupations but prevocational and postvocational activities and decisions as well as how persons integrate their work life with their other life roles such as family, community and leisure pursuits. A career may include many occupations and jobs" (Ettinger 1996). More simply, Ross (1995) described a career as the "sum of a person's experiences over the course of a lifetime," and reinforced the notion that career needs are interwoven with personal and social needs. "This concept recognizes that our jobs don't exist in isolation from the rest of our lives. In a single career, someone may have been a student, a plumber, an engineering technologist, a mother and a semi-retired consultant" (Ross 1995). This is in contrast to the definition of a *job,* which has been defined as "a group of similar paid positions requiring some similar attributes in a single organization" (Super 1976 as cited in Herr and Cramer 1996). These definitions portray a career as more personal than jobs held or the occupations in which an individual has been involved.

One of the challenges that career centers face is that of increasing user understanding of what now comprises the career development process. "The narrow definitions of career as job and of career planning as fitting into a job—the old linear model—are often still used. It is hard to change the mindset. In this scenario, people scan the environment for information and compete for their piece of a limited pie rather than see multiple possibilities in themselves and in society, in work and in all of life's roles" (Hansen 1997). As the definition of a career has expanded, so has the complexity of career development. These complexities challenge the perceptions and expectations of many providers and users within career development service delivery systems.

Career development has been defined as "the process by which one develops and refines self- and career-identity, work maturity and the ability to plan. It represents all the career-related choices and outcomes through which every person must pass. Indeed career development is generally conceived as a lifelong process through which individuals come to understand themselves as they relate to the world of work and their role in it" (Schilling, Schwallie-Giddis, and Giddis 1995). Gysbers (1996) expanded the definition to include the life roles outside of the workplace because career development

> . . . is a lens through which clients can view and understand work and family concerns. Add the factors of gender, ethnic origin, race, and religion and the lens becomes even more powerful. Now clients have a way of bringing their personal histories and the histories of their reference groups into focus. Now they can see how these factors have directly or indirectly influenced them, their views of themselves, others, and the world in which they live. Now they have four additional factors to use to understand and respond to their struggles with work and family issues and concerns.

Herr and Cramer (1996) reinforced both the progressive nature of career development and the crucial role of envisioning career development from the perspective of the individual rather than from the narrow job placement perspective:

> [Career development includes] the lifelong behavioral processes and the influences on them that lead to one's work values, choice of occupation(s), creation of a career pattern, decision-making style, role integration, self-identity and career identity, educational literacy, and related phenomena. Career development proceeds— smoothly, jaggedly, positively, negatively—whether or not career guidance or career education exists. As such, career development is not an intervention but the object of an intervention.

While these definitions clarify the foundational concepts, they also guide the development of programs and services for career centers. One of the challenges that career centers face in their development is disputing perceptual barriers that view career development as the process of finding that first, single job. That perception leads to career centers that only provide information and guidance in finding the "perfect fit" between skills and jobs, ignoring life roles, continuous learning, and the responsibility of individuals in their career development processes. Borchard (1995) provided some insight into historical factors and the related attitudinal barriers that might influence an individual's approach to career development (and thereby influence their expectations of career centers). This information can be useful in helping individuals to recognize and consider how transitions in the world of work impact personal definitions of career and career development.

Borchard (1995) suggested that society is currently in a transition period between the end of one era (the Mass Production Era, which began in 1865 and ended in the 1980s) and the beginning of the next era (the Knowledge-Service Era, which started in the 1980s and extends to the present time). "The structural changes engulfing us over the past couple of decades have transformed our world from a corporation-centered and manufacturing-based order (the Mass Production Era) to that of a predominantly service-based, technology- and information-driven system (the Knowledge-Service Era)" (Borchard 1995). He suggested that the changing economy and changing work environment have placed different demands on future employees than were placed on previous generations. These changing demands have a widespread impact.

- The job-market structure has changed from a two-tiered factory system where blue-collar workers were dominated by white-collar workers (and some K-12 schools were organized to prepare students for one of two options—go to college or go to work) to a system of multitiered (or no tiered) structures where discussions of "gold collar workers" who possess a combination of technical competence and conceptual knowledge are increasing (for which the school-to-work movement is attempting to prepare students).

- The source for employment has shifted from one organization for the entire work life to multiple employers over an individual's career.
- The few stable, classifiable types of occupational characteristics are being replaced by many rapidly evolving occupational characteristics.
- It used to be that individuals completed their education (at whatever level) and went to work; increasingly, there has been a shift to continuous learning over the lifespan, particularly considering the rapid, continuous growth of technology.
- In the past, people got jobs through family ties (blue-collar) or through classified ads and resumes (white-collar). In the Knowledge-Service Era, however, developing individual skills and competencies and ongoing networking are becoming more important.
- Career choices now are reached less through luck and happenstance and more through decision making and ongoing attention to the changing workplace.

(Condensed from Borchard 1995)

In addition to these well-noted shifts in the economy, it has also been indicated that the next shift in the economy has been developing since the late 1990's and into the early 2000's. It has been described as the "Intangible Economy" also described as the "I-Cubed Economy" (Information, Innovation, Intangibles). Goldfinger (1998) suggested that "the advent of an 'intangible' economy does not mean the end of work. But it does mean the end of familiar routines and rhythms, of job security, of rigid hierarchies and career planning." He points to the increase in part-time, temporary, and flex-time work along with short-term contracts as symbols of this new economy. The ability to acknowledge and respond to the ongoing changes in the world of work, including emerging technologies and economic trends, in a timely manner is vital.

Two major elements arise from the comparison of career development in the Mass Production Era to career development in the Knowledge-Service Era and beyond that should be highlighted for both users and staff in career centers.

First, there is the contrast between the organization controlling (or guiding) the career development process for the individual and the individual managing her or his own career. The implication is that as individuals assume the role of career manager, they need direction and assistance different from that provided in the past, when the emphasis was on finding a single job.

Second, this transition from the old era to the new one highlights the importance of individuals' ability to identify skills and transfer them from one environment to another. This becomes critical as individuals look to enter or progress in the workplace. Individuals demonstrate that capacity by reviewing experiences, identifying the skills developed through those experiences, and then applying those skills to new situations. Career centers can contribute by

- teaching the process of skill identification and transferability of skills to multiple environments (and jobs),
- creating opportunities through collaborative agreements with employers or service organizations through which individuals can explore jobs/occupations and test their skills, and
- encouraging individuals to learn and then practice the skills they identify as important to the future.

Career centers can impact their communities by confronting the perceptual boundaries through education and the development of programs/services that represent a broader approach to career development.

A simpler way to characterize the career development process at the individual level is to view career development as the ongoing, overlapping process of seeking the answers to three questions: *Who am I?*, *Where am I going?*, and *How do I get there?* (Figure 1). This

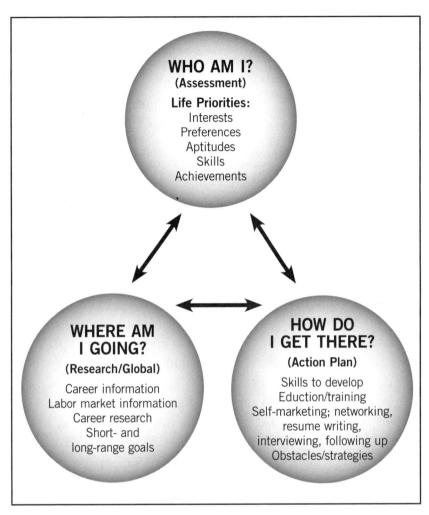

FIGURE 1.1: Three Critical Questions

graphic captures the essence of the career development process. The *Who am I?* component encourages individuals to consider the personal characteristics brought to the process. The *Where am I going?* component involves the gathering, consolidation, and synthesis of information from the world of work with personal characteristics. Those two components combine and are projected into the future through the *How do I get there?* planning component.

In the Mass Production Era, career development consisted primarily of *Where am I going?* and *How do I get there?*, and the process ended once one arrived at the work experience. In the Knowledge-Service Era, the circle represents recycling through the process of answering the three questions. This continuous loop of self-knowledge (Who am I?), educational and occupational exploration (Where am I going?), and career planning (How do I get there?) is also supported and specified more thoroughly in the National Career Development competencies and indicators.

The National Career Development Guidelines (NCDG) were developed by the National Occupational Information Coordinating Committee (NOICC) in 1989 to stimulate state and local communities to create comprehensive career development programs. In 2003, the U.S. Department of Education's Office of Vocational and Adult Education (OVAE) commissioned a revision of the guidelines. The guidelines are "a framework for thinking about the knowledge and skills young people and adults need to manage their careers effectively, from making decisions about school to taking that first job and beyond" (ACRN, 2006). The revision was also intended to support educators and schools working toward success as defined by the No Child Left Behind Act of 2001 (Public Law 107-110), commonly known as NCLB. Provided with the guidelines are activities and supporting materials to assist professionals in the design and delivery of career development programs.

The Guidelines are divided into three content domains: Personal Social Development, Educational Achievement and Lifelong Learning, and Career Management. Under each domain are goals that define broad areas of career development competency. The domains and competencies are (ACRN, 2006):

Personal Social Development Domain
• Develop understanding of self to build and maintain a positive self-concept.

- Develop positive interpersonal skills including respect for diversity.
- Integrate growth and change into your career development.
- Balance personal, leisure, community, learner, family, and work roles.

Educational Achievement and Lifelong Learning Domain

- Attain educational achievement and performance levels needed to reach your personal and career goals.
- Participate in ongoing, lifelong learning experiences to enhance your ability to function effectively in a diverse and changing economy.

Career Management Domain

- Create and manage a career plan that meets your career goals.
- Use a process of decision-making as one component of career development.
- Use accurate, current, and unbiased career information during career planning and management.
- Master academic, occupational, and general employability skills in order to obtain, create, maintain, and/or advance your employment.
- Integrate changing employment trends, societal needs, and economic conditions into your career plans.

In addition, each goal also provides indicators related to the knowledge and skills needed to achieve that goal. The indicators are further described relative to three stages of learning: knowledge acquisition, application, and reflection. The National Career Development Guidelines Web site (http://www.acrnetwork.org/ncdg/) is an excellent resource, complete with online activities for each goal.

While it is important for career centers to connect to national initiatives like the NCDG, there may also be state, local, or population-specific models that can be used to provide direction and support to the development and implementation of the career center. Many states have developmental guidance models through which school counseling programs work with teachers to provide activities that help students progress in specific developmental areas. For example, the state of Wisconsin has a developmental guidance model consisting of nine competency areas that suggest that students can: connect family, school, and work; solve problems; understand diversity, inclusiveness, and fairness; work in groups; manage conflict; integrate growth and development; direct change; make decisions; and set and achieve goals (Schutt, Brittingham, Perrone, Bilzing, and Thompson 1997).

A clear conceptualization of career and career development is important when developing programs and services in career centers. Centers can work with individuals to organize these concepts (particularly the answers to *Who am I?*, *Where am I going?*, and *How do I get there?*) through the creation and maintenance of an individual career plan. Career plans that are developed individually and represent the career development process can be useful in encouraging center users to become managers of their own career development.

Career plans are developed in many ways and come in a variety of forms. Portfolio-planners illustrate one form that is often used by schools but just as frequently overlooked by adults. Portfolios are useful in providing structure to the career development process and can direct individuals through the following steps:

- Guide individuals through identifying their skills, interests, and abilities.
- Encourage them to process that information to identify occupational areas that might be of interest.
- Have them investigate the occupations, paying particular attention to skill areas that they might need to enhance if they wish to pursue a particular occupational area.

- Once a choice has been identified, encourage them to use the planning component to search for a workplace experience to "test" out a job in the occupational area.
- Depending on the outcome of the experience, plot a course for entry detailed through the portfolio-planner.
- Continuously return to the portfolio-planner to update success and project new areas necessary to continue growing, developing, and preparing for the changing world of work. (NOICC 1996)

Again, portfolio-planners are but one of the many tools that can be created to respond to the changing demands in the workplace. Regardless of form, the plans should help individuals to synthesize the information needed to make effective decisions about the development of their careers. Viewing career development as a lifelong process directs the type of information that needs to be gathered and the consideration it needs to be given. An excellent online article with resources is provided by the National Education Association (2006) and can be found at http://www.nea.org/lessons/2004/tt040614.html (available as of April 2007.

In general, career centers can assist individuals in making career decisions and developing plans that consolidate past experiences, identify existing personal (likes, dislikes, interests, skills, abilities, past work successes, and aptitudes) and situational (family demands, economic needs, geographic preferences, future dreams) variables, and use this information to chart a course for the future that examines skills and interests applicable across possibly many different jobs or occupations. While the outcome might be individuals naming a single job or occupational area, the goal should be to help them identify a number of opportunities and to integrate lifelong learning into the plan.

IMPLICATIONS FOR CAREER CENTERS

From the previous discussion, five implications emerge as career centers look to engage in providing services.

1. *There is a critical need to educate staff, advisory boards, and users on the changing needs of individuals relative to career development.* Although it has become evident that career development must be a self-directed, lifelong process, this still has not been incorporated into the training of many career professionals and the operations of many career centers. They are still operating according to the old linear model of assessing skills and matching them with job openings.

   It is important to challenge that model because to work oblivious to the modern definition of career development as a lifelong process may adversely affect the services offered and ultimately the lives of center users. McDaniels and Gysbers (1992) addressed this more specifically when they noted the problem of individual assessments made in the traditional model seeking to predict which educational or employment opportunities would be most suitable. While prediction must remain a part of the modern career development process, it must be supplemented by methods of exploring and expanding all of the individual's interests and abilities.

2. *Keep the goals and objectives of the center consistent with the goals and objectives of career development.* Remember that "careers are unique to each person and created by what one chooses or does not choose. They are dynamic and unfold throughout life. They include not only occupations but prevocational and postvocational concerns as well as integration of work with other roles: family, community, leisure" (Herr and Cramer 1996). Provide services beyond the traditional individual assessments, career and labor market information, and placement. Teach career development processes and reiterate the individual's need for continuously answering the three questions of *Who am I?*, *Where am I going?*, and *How do I get there?* Regardless of the setting of your career center, the goals and objectives

must also be kept in line with those of the institution to which you are connected, either physically or financially.

3. *Be clear as to what the center can and cannot offer.* Do not mislead users by suggesting that the services provided are comprehensive if they are not. If the center can offer assessment services and career information, for example, it should make clear to its users that they are not receiving placement assistance and then refer them to centers that do help with placement. Likewise, if the center cannot offer Internet access it should make users aware of these resources and suggest where they might go to take advantage of them. Simple decency demands that centers be honest with their users, but this kind of honesty about the range of services offered also leads users to form realistic expectations and expand their knowledge of what is available to them.

4. *Teach individuals to become managers of their own career development process.* As the pattern of determining one's career has changed, so must the ownership of the career development process. In the past, it was permissible for individuals to find one job and let their employer direct their careers from then on. That simply does not happen today. Employees no longer feel tied to their employers and employers no longer direct the careers of their employees; as Hansen (1997) noted, "the most frequent estimate is that the average adult will make five to seven major career changes in a lifetime." Clearly, individuals need to take charge of their own career development and take action to ensure that their needs and desires are met, their abilities and interests put to good use. Career centers can support this by providing the tools that individuals need to make fully informed, workable decisions at every stage of their lives.

5. *Create tools such as an individualized personal career plan.* Employing career plans as a method for individuals to steer

their paths is consistent with the career development process being managed at the individual level. Formalize the process as well as the tools for use with the center's intended audience, recognizing their needs and the developmental level (using the NCDG and other modern guidelines as a gauge) at which they enter the system. Regardless of your target audience or your experience in career center development, it is important to consult with other career centers to gain a deeper understanding of how these processes and tools can work. If your center does not have the resources necessary to offer the construction of individual career plans (or similar tools), it is best to work with other centers or contract with other professionals to provide them.

CAREER CENTERS AND CAREER DEVELOPMENT

The specific role of career centers relative to career development is left ultimately to the developer of the center. While the specifics are yet to be determined, there are common themes that should run through centers.

Career centers should serve as facilitators of the career development process. Most importantly, the services offered and the method of use should teach individuals the process of learning about themselves and the world of work, challenging old paradigms of their role in that world. It is important to teach new processes (answering the three questions) not used or necessarily understood by many adults who entered the world of work during the Mass Production Era. Their experiences—and the experiences of their role models—may not reflect existing realities. For example, an adult may have used family connections to secure a position at the same company where his or her relatives worked. If the company closes, that person is not only unemployed but also limited by his or her solitary, outmoded concept of how to pursue a career. Such an adult could greatly benefit from a career center intervening to teach the career development process (including the concept of lifelong learning) as a part of the effort to assist in finding new work. By teaching the process, the career center meets the immediate needs to find work while also preparing the individual for future job transitions over the course of his or her career.

Another related theme is the synthesis of information used to make career decisions and to develop career plans. At one time, access to information was a critical issue. With the advent of the Internet and other methods of quickly transmitting large quantities of information, however, the problem is no longer one of access but of managing the information to make sense of it on a personal level. Career centers can teach individuals how to use new technologies to gather information and, more importantly, consolidate and personalize the information to meet the individuals' career development needs. Only after determining what those needs are and how the individuals' interests and abilities come into play can centers really help clients determine what career and labor market information is relevant and useful.

Finally, career centers can serve as resource centers for their communities. Partnership and collaborative projects should be developed to connect the center with others contributing to the career development of individuals in the community. This can help to identify new contributors, to garner support for the center, and ultimately to connect center users with the world of work.

It is both interesting and important to note that each of the varied and meaningful roles the career center plays is always a supporting role. Career centers can and do make a real difference in the lives of those who seek help and guidance at various stages of their careers. Still, it must be stated that the individual clients bear ultimate responsibility for their career choices and the results—good and bad—their decisions bring.

SUMMARY

Conceptual Components

- A career is the sequence of occupational and leisure activities unique to each person.

- A job is just a paid position or a group of similar paid positions.
- Career development is the lifelong process of career and personal decision-making.
- The Mass Production Era (1865 to the 1980s) was marked by single, stable careers guided by employers.
- The Knowledge-Service Era (the 1980s to the present) is marked by multiple, diverse careers guided by employees.
- The "Intangible Economy" brings new routines and rhythms.

The career development process of the individual can be characterized as the ongoing process of asking the following questions:

- Who am I?
- Where am I going?
- How do I get there?

Implications for Career Centers

- Recognize the critical need to educate staff, advisory boards, and users on the changing career development needs of individuals.
- Keep the goals and objectives of the center consistent with the goals and objectives of career development.
- Be clear as to what the center can and cannot offer.
- Teach individuals to become managers of their own career development processes.
- Create tools such as an individualized personal career plan.

CHAPTER 2

Program Planning, Assessment, and Evaluation: Understanding Who You Serve

by Donald A. Schutt Jr.

Determining who your center serves is a vital question to answer in the beginning stages of development. It impacts logistical questions such as location and hours of service as well as the method of delivering services. Exploring the needs of your audience and assessing the environment in which the center exists allows you to create goals that reflect the purpose of the center. Assessment and evaluation is an important process to continuously weave into all center activities; however, by regularly revisiting the question of service to the target audience, you can adapt the center to keep pace with a changing world and the changing needs of your clients.

This chapter looks at program planning, assessment and evaluation as a continuous planning and improvement process for career centers. Commonly, this process is seen as having a distinct beginning and ending (which is different than will be discussed here). As such, needs assessments are discussed at the beginning of development and evaluation is seen as the finale to the implementation process. However, when discussed as a planning and improvement process, both assessment and evaluation are closely connected, so that data can be collected continuously and used as a method for ongoing program planning and improvement.

Prior to beginning the planning and improvement process, it may be useful to explore already established models. The value in identifying and using existing planning and improvement models while developing your career center's approach is three-fold: savings in resources such as staff time and energy; opportunities to use time- and field-tested criteria that allow you to measure your career center against other organizations; and lastly, using existing models offers a common language for sharing best practices. One such example are the Baldrige Criteria for Performance Excellence (http://www.quality.nist.gov/Criteria.htm) which the National Association of College and University Business Officers (NACUBO) used to develop an Excellence in Higher Education (EHE) framework (Ruben 2005) that has potential for application to career centers. The EHE framework grouped questions into seven categories focused on areas that contribute to organizational effectiveness as well as areas that provided documentation of outcomes and achievements. The categories were:

1. Leadership
2. Strategic planning
3. Beneficiaries and constituencies
4. Programs and services
5. Faculty, staff, and workplace
6. Assessment and information use
7. Outcomes and achievements (Ruben 2005 pp. 11–12)

These categories would then be woven into the planning and improvement process.

Splete and Freed (2006), drawing on the Baldridge and two other certification systems, found these common key features:

- an organizational structure reflecting mission and purpose
- identified core values and principles
- performance standards based on values and principles

- detailed framework for self-assessment
- a third-party review system
- written feedback
- technical assistance and training (Splete & Freed 2006)

From these findings, they created "High Performance Career Development Programming standards (HPCD) focusing on self-assessment and Centers of Excellence procedures" (Splete & Freed 2006). The HPCD was piloted in eight organizations and expanded to more than 30 program teams through the Career Development Program Network of Southwestern PA (CDPN) (http://www.cdpn.net). The progression of this pilot as well as for more information on Centers of Career Development Excellence (CoE) Program Accreditation, see http://www.wdpn.net/excellencecert.html.

The planning and improvement process begins with (1) needs assessment, which leads to (2) program planning, followed by (3) formative or process evaluation, and ending with (4) summative or outcome evaluation (Isaac and Michael 1984). These four steps continuously loop back to reviewing the needs of users and how the center can improve on delivering services to meet those needs (see Figure 2).

It is important to begin the development of the center with the end in mind. In other words, decide early on what the center needs to understand about its users and services, and then build a process that will provide the answers to those questions while maintaining the flexibility to respond in a timely fashion to feedback and patterns not anticipated.

THE NEEDS ASSESSMENT

The purpose of a needs assessment is to identify the issues from which the career center's mission, operating principles, vision, and goals emerge. Isaac and Michael support this purpose: "A need has been defined as the discrepancy between what is and what ought to be. Once identified, needs are placed in order of priority. They are

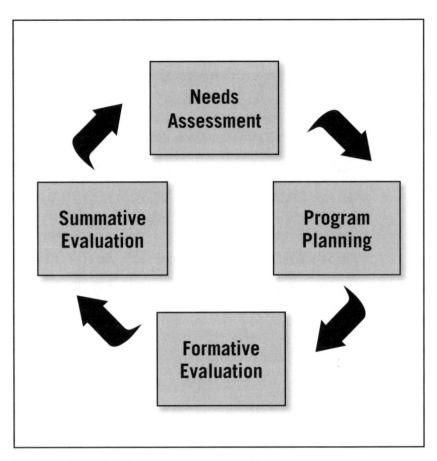

FIGURE 2: The Planning and Improvement Process

the basis for setting program goals" (1984). Often, identified needs represent problems or challenges to be overcome, problems which could come in many forms.

Take as a simple but all too common example a college student who decides to be an elementary school teacher. As an undergraduate, she majors in education. During the student's senior year practice teaching, a problem arises when she realizes that working with young children is not to her liking. This problem might have been averted if the campus career center and the advising office had worked together to suggest that students explore potential majors through experiences in the workplace prior to making firm decisions. An even better solution would have been for the career center to establish relationships with employers or alumni in order to provide sites at which students could meet those exploratory needs. This problem or need, transformed to a program goal, might lead the center to develop closer working relationships with existing campus departments that provide students with advising related to occupational or career goals.

The National Career Development Guidelines (NCDG) provide a framework for better understanding the *what ought to be*. While the guidelines focus on creating comprehensive career development programs through competencies and indicators (discussed in Chapter 1). The earlier NCDG detailed three programs areas: content, processes, and structure (NOICC 1985b). While the content is now represented in the three content domains, 11 competencies, and associated goals of the revised NCDG (2006), the processes and structure program areas are still useful. *Processes* are the strategies that actually deliver the program content, and *structure* is the framework supporting the programs' activities. The structure includes organizing the planning of the program, clarifying staff roles and responsibilities, securing resources, monitoring program delivery, and revising the program.

NCDG Program Components

Program Delivery Processes:
    Outreach
    Instruction
    Counseling
    Assessment
    Career information
    Work experience
    Placement
    Consultation
    Referral
    Follow-up

Program Structure:
Leadership
Program Management
Personnel
Facilities
Resources
(NOICC 1995b)

These program areas provide career centers with a framework to understand *what ought to be* in place as well as a strategy for organizing components within a program. These areas also translate to the operation of a career center as they address the questions of (1) What are we delivering (content)? (2) How is that content going to be delivered (processes)? and (3) How will we achieve this within our organizational structure (structure)?

The program content areas and the program delivery processes draw directly from the needs assessment discussed in this section. Initially, the center's leadership and program management structure may already be in place as the needs assessment process begins (in fact, they may be responsible for the process). The needs assessment serves to clarify issues related to the delivery process, staffing requirements, facilities, and resources required to complete the center. A thorough assessment of the needs of the community (or environment) and of the individual user provides the foundation for the center.

Identifying Community and Environment Issues

What is known about the environment where the career center will be located? Are other services currently offered in the community? Are those services offered to some people but not to others? Is there support for the career center or is it seen as competing with existing services or programs? Who will collaborate with the center to create a seamless system of delivery? In schools is there a developmental guidance program that has a career component in place? Who has access and who needs access to the services a career center can provide? While some career centers are established to meet specific demands within a community (like students making the transitions from education to employment or civilians readjusting after military base closures), other centers operate to serve the needs of entire cities and counties. Regardless of the context, it is important to have a sense of the role the center plays in the community.

The community and environment components to be assessed include: attitudes about career centers; political climate in the community regarding career development; number of community-based organizations, technical colleges, or other organizations providing services; resources available internally and externally, and the ability to collaborate with school programs (even for centers serving populations other than K-12 students). It also includes questions of access to and support from local business partners, postsecondary educational institutions, other training programs, and various community agencies.

Gysbers and Henderson (1994) provided one example of a community and environment assessment that demonstrated an exhaustive process for schools to follow when developing a comprehensive developmental school guidance program. While their example was directed at developing a school guidance program, there is significant overlap between that endeavor and the task of developing a comprehensive career center. The advice of Gysbers and Henderson is worth noting:

> The efficiency of a program is measured in terms of the ratio of resources applied to the benefits accrued. Thus, gathering concrete information about the resources available and used in the guidance program is essential to any program decisions to be made. The more complete your knowledge of the resources currently available, the more room you have for creativity as you decide to redirect them for program improvements and the more specific you can be in your requests for additional resources.

They went on to define resources in three different areas: human, financial, and political. In the area of human resources, they studied student-to-counselor ratios and provided a succinct description of a counselor time study used to evaluate the allotment of time appropriated to each of four counseling program task areas. Those areas had been identified earlier in the process as comprising the counseling program content area. The financial resources were identified as budget expenditures, existing materials and equipment, and facilities, so they were prepared in case additional space was needed for workshops or other activities. The political resources evaluated were policy statements made at the school, district, community, state, and federal levels. From this assessment, gaps were identified and a determination was made regarding the support that could be expected as the program advanced through the development and planning stages.

Assessing the community climate for potential collaboration with and support for the center needs to be given high consideration as goals are developed. Of equal importance is gaining insights into the services that potential users currently need as well as predicting the services that users might request once the center is available.

Understanding Individual Needs

The career needs of individuals are diverse. As the workforce becomes older, and more diverse in terms of gender, racial and ethnic composition, the approaches that career centers take must keep pace. As was mentioned in the previous chapter, diversity also exists in the ways that people approach their careers, as well as the issues that have become a part of career development dialogues. Whether it is shifting from full-time to part-time work to accommodate child or elder care, or the increase in dual-career partners, or the shift toward multilingualism in the workplace, career centers need to be prepared to understand the emerging needs. Clarifying the gaps in existing services and exploring the possibilities for services never before considered are included in the assessment of individual needs. While the previous assessment of the community and environment entailed a consideration of attitudes, resources, and connections, the assessment of individual needs focuses on who the center's users are and what they want. Brown and Brown (1990) recommended that individual needs assessment be designed to collect information in the following areas:

1. whether there is a desire for assistance with career planning;
2. preferred type of assistance with career planning (e.g., individual counseling);
3. types of career information needed; and
4. special need[s].

The first area, "desire for assistance with career planning," focused on how many people expect to access the career center. It also set out to provide an estimate of when individuals might participate if various types of career development activities were offered. Interest in participating in career development programming should be elicited during the needs assessment. Questions that might help generate this type of information are: Are you interested in exploring career opportunities at this time? Are you planning to use a career center to explore career opportunities within the next three months? Six months? Determining the desire for career assistance achieves two goals. One, of course, is whether individuals would consider coming to a career center to explore career opportunities. The second, perhaps not as obvious a goal, is to provoke the thought in individuals that a career center is a resource for meeting their career development needs.

The second area, "preferred types of assistance," gauged individuals' preferred delivery process. Brown and Brown (1990) suggested that potential users should be queried with regard to the manner they would prefer to access career development services. Examples included individual career counseling, group career exploration activities, and self-directed activities such as using a computer. This is directly connected to the processes that the center envisions in terms of service delivery. Through this assessment, it might be discovered that there is no interest in working in groups but great interest in individual counseling, and this will shape the type of services the center will provide.

"Types of career information needed" was the third area. This required a better understanding of the specific reasons for a user to come to the center. Are they seeking information about a particular occupation? Perhaps they want to know what the demand will be for a given occupation five years from now. Employing the three content areas from the National Career Development Guidelines, it might be possible to stimulate user interest in investigating the other two areas of self-knowledge or career planning (in addition to the area related to educational and occupational information that brought them to the center). This also provides an opportunity to educate individuals with the Mass Production Era view of career development about the changing nature of workplaces and approaches to career development.

Lastly, "identifying special needs" refers to necessary adaptations in the center with such items as adapted computer screens, captioned video and computer segments, desk heights that facilitate wheel chair access, assistance in retrieving materials from shelves, or restrooms with accessible stalls. This area addresses questions of access and user-oriented services. Special needs might also include bilingual staff, or staff familiar with issues related to second-generation students. These special needs might also direct the types of resources and services that a center offers based on the types of information sought by different groups.

Identifying and understanding how to respond to many different needs posed by the variety of individual developmental career needs is challenging. A basic student needs survey should collect individual information in five different areas: academic needs, career, special topics, preferred activities, and comments. Carefully determine the individual information needed to help build a profile of potential users of the career center and consider how that information fits with the results of the community and environmental assessment. Career center staff should determine what the priority is—individual needs, community needs, or both—and then shape the center based on those priorities.

Collecting Information (Data Collection)

There are many different ways to collect data. The methods used to gather data typically either expand the breadth of knowledge regarding a topic or seek to deepen understanding. Planning the data collection process is critical as it ensures that the information collected is both useful and thorough. One format for planning the needs assessment is:

1. Identify the participants.
   Which groups will be assessed?
   How will these groups be sampled?
   Based on expected return, how many people do we need to have in the sample?
2. Finalize the needs assessment method.
   Does the recommended needs assessment instrument meet our needs? If not, how should it be modified?
   What alternative forms do we want to develop for specific groups?
   Will respondents be willing to respond to the entire instrument or should we divide the competencies into two instruments?
   How should we format the instrument so it is easy to score?
3. Collect data.
   How will the instruments be administered? Will we use a different approach for different groups?
   Who will be responsible for administering the instrument to each group?
   What is our time schedule for administration?
   How many follow-ups will we do? When should they be done? How will we do them?

4. Analyze data.

How will we determine what competencies and indicators were rated most and least important?

How will we determine whether the results differed by group?

How can we report the results to various groups?

(Condensed from Kobylarz 1996)

This example provides general tips for developing a plan to assess and evaluate the competencies and indicators as a measure of individual needs. The assumption, while not explicit, is that a paper-and-pencil instrument or electronic survey will be administered. Brown and Brown (1990) suggested the following process for conducting an assessment based on a needs assessment questionnaire:

1. Use a committee that is generally familiar with the potential users of the [career center] to draft the questionnaire. Include some of the potential users (e.g., students, employees) on the committee.
2. Field test the questionnaire to make sure that questions are understood and provide the data needed.
3. When possible, use answer sheets that can be scanned and tabulated by a computer to save time.
4. Keep the questionnaire as short as possible. The longer the questionnaire, the lower the return rate.
5. Disseminate the information to potential users of the [career center:] counselors, managers/administrators, and others who have a need to know.
6. Rank the needs as one means of establishing priorities for the center. Typically, needs are ranked on the basis of the number of people expressing a need (e.g., 100 people want more information about high-tech occupations), but the needs of minorities, women, and the physically handicapped should receive high priority.

(Brown and Brown 1990)

The distinction between these two examples is a focus on the content of the instrument or program under development in the first example and a focus on a process for developing the assessment in the other (Brown and Brown). Both of these examples describe data collection procedures that collect a breadth of information that can be analyzed to find patterns from which individual needs can be identified.

When the plan calls for a greater depth of information, interviews, focus groups and informal conversations are useful data collection methods. The advantages of each must be considered along with limitations, but thorough planning and preparation increases the effectiveness of any data collection method.

Interviews can be formally structured, or they can be open-ended and nondirect. The advantage of interviews is that they are flexible and can result in a greater understanding of participant responses. For example, a survey of a broad community audience may reveal that 95 percent of potential center users feel isolated during a job search. However, interviews focusing on depth would allow respondents to explain what "isolated" means to them. For one person it might mean an extended delay sitting in an employer's reception area. For another, it might mean long evenings alone writing cover letters. Disadvantages of interviews include the fact that they take longer to conduct, data analysis can be challenging, and variation in interviewer skills may produce inconsistent results.

Focus group sessions are an efficient means to gather individual information, particularly as related to investment of time. Focus groups also allow for a natural synergy to occur among participants resulting in more meaningful information than if individual interviews were conducted with each person. Two drawbacks of this type of method include the high skill level needed by session facilitators and the difficulty of performing data analysis.

A third, often overlooked method is dialogues with colleagues, friends, family, and acquaintances. This informal approach calls for identifying and communicating with those people in the community who are well connected and who can provide insight into a variety of needs. This notion of using insights from the community is not a new one; Knowles (1978) suggested that opinions of experts and people in helping roles be sought to identify needs they perceive as widespread among potential participants.

The purpose in gathering information is to begin to identify areas where career centers can have an impact either by enhancing existing services or by revealing new opportunities. In consolidating the data into a report, consider analyzing the need or problem. The following questions assist in formulating a response or goal:

1. What is the problem or need identified? (Summarize it in a sentence.)
2. What is happening? (Describe the present situation.)
3. What should be happening? (Describe applicable standards, objectives, policies.)
4. What is the gap between what is happening and what should be happening? (Explain it as precisely as possible.)
5. How important is the difference between what is happening and what should be happening? (Describe costs of the problem or consequences if left unattended, as well as you can anticipate them.)
6. What causes the difference between what is happening and what should be happening? (Describe briefly whether it is caused by a deficiency in knowledge, skills, or the environment.)
7. What is the appropriate solution to the problem? (Explain how the career center can meet the need identified.)
8. What will be the likely impact of the solution on the community or organization? (Describe possible positive and negative consequences of any proposed solution and then explain how to head off the negative consequences.)

(Adapted from Rothwell and Kazanas 1992)

By systematically applying these questions, a goal statement can be developed that addresses the opportunities and needs to which the career center will respond. Ultimately, the mission of the center along with programmatic goals should be developed and prioritized through the needs assessment process.

PROGRAM PLANNING

The words *mission, purpose* and *role* are often used interchangeably to describe this first step in the planning process. The needs assessment, including the data collection, provided the foundation for the mission statement. Effective mission statements inspire change, are long-term, easy to understand, and communicate to others (Niven 2002). Letters & Science/Human Ecology Career Services at University of Wisconsin-Madison has a very clear mission statement:

> To educate and support Letters and Science/Human Ecology students with their career development process, enabling them to integrate their academic and life experiences with their career goals and transition to the world of work. (http://www.lssaa.wisc.edu/careers/about/mission.php retrieved April 22, 2007)

The mission statement is supported by an expanded purpose statement:

> In order to facilitate our mission, the Letters and Science/Human Ecology Career Service office exists to do the following:
> - To advise and assist Letters and Science/Human Ecology students and recent alumni with:
>   - self-assessment
>   - career exploration
>   - decision making
>   - planning and implementing job search and
>   - to assist students with making decisions about how graduate school fits in with their career path

- We encourage active student participation in planning and implementing our programs and value student's voices and suggestions regarding our services.
- To provide a richer experience for our students, we actively partner and collaborate with campus constituencies, community, alumni and employers.
- To provide students with a variety of connections with employers to position them for success after graduation.
  (http://www.lssaa.wisc.edu/careers/about/mission.php
  retrieved April 22, 2007)

A clear definition of mission is a prerequisite to planning for a career center. While there is no standard way to write a mission statement, these elements are often included:

- Why—The main reason for the career center to exist
- What—The products or services
- Who—The customer, client, consumer, or market served
- Where—The primary scope and/or boundaries of the organization

Goals are "broadly philosophical, global, relatively timeless, and nonmeasurable" (Isaac and Michael 1984) statements about center activities, services, or processes. The program planning phase expands on the goals also created from the needs assessment.

Program planning responds with action to the goals developed through the needs assessment. "From program goals, specific measurable objectives are derived and a plan containing the means to attain these objectives—the program procedures, strategies, and activities—is formulated" (Isaac and Michael 1984). Simply put, "the evaluation of the [center] actually begins when the objectives (1) address a need, (2) tell what program is to be employed to meet that need, (3) identify a date by which the program is to be completed, and (4) establish a criterion for success" (Brown and Brown 1990).

One level of specificity among goals and objectives was demonstrated in this excerpt from a report on the development of a high school career center.

Expected Outcomes

1. Fifty of the one hundred high school teachers will sign out materials from the career education resource center.
2. Fifty of the one hundred teachers will write a summary of how the career education center materials assisted their classroom lessons.
3. Seventy of one hundred randomly selected seniors will indicate a college major or career direction on their final plans.

Measurement of Outcome

1. Over a 12 week period a circulation record will show that 50 of the one hundred high school teachers have used the career education center to obtain materials for their classroom lessons.
2. Over a 12 week period 50 of the one hundred high school teachers will write a summary of how they used the career education materials to improve their classroom lessons.
3. At the end of the 12-week period, when presented with a survey, 70 of one hundred randomly selected seniors will be able to indicate either a college major or career direction on their final plans.

(Adapted from Zalinsky 1993)

In this particular program, these outcome statements directed the development of the program down to the forms for keeping records, including the follow-up surveys to teachers.

Once the objectives have been defined, intervention strategies, activities, and delivery processes should be identified. Choosing the most appropriate strategy for achieving the goals and meeting the objectives requires consideration for the instructional mode used to facilitate the career development process. Many choices exist in terms of delivery, from face-to-face individual contacts to groups and from distance education to computer-based training. The following questions can guide centers toward selecting an effective mode (or modes) of instruction.

1. How do the performance objectives connect to the content?
2. What basic instructional strategies (or processes) do you think would be most suitable for achieving these objectives with the people you will be working with, taking account of all relevant factors?
3. Which processes should be adopted: outreach, instruction, counseling, assessment, career information, work experience, placement, consultation, or referral?
4. Of these processes, which does the center have the capacity to provide given the materials, facilities, and staff?

Centers may be prevented from providing some of these services by staff composition. In cases where the most effective instructional mode is not available at the center, it is the ethical responsibility of the center to refer the user to a qualified service provider.

The needs assessment should lead to the development of the program goals and objectives that are linked to the activities proposed by the center. These activities, connected to the three broad career development content areas of self-knowledge, educational and occupational exploration, and career planning, will also have been combined in the program planning stage with delivery processes that are within the perimeter of the center's capacity. It is at this stage that the career center is shifting into the implementation mode, and there is an ongoing assessment and evaluation of the overall program.

FORMATIVE EVALUATION

Formative (sometimes referred to as *proactive* or *process*) evaluation is concerned with formulating an evaluation of instruction/delivery to facilitate ongoing program improvement and planning. In the formative evaluation process, both the progress toward the earlier identified objectives and the implementation should be evaluated. According to Isaac and Michael (1984), the evaluation of the implementation "seeks out discrepancies between the plan and the reality [and] keeps the program true to its design or modifies it appropriately." The evaluation of the process is distinguished from the evaluation of the outcomes as it "monitors indicators of progress [developed in the program planning stage] toward the objectives; makes mid-course corrections, as appropriate." The method of evaluation may take many forms, similar to those discussed in the data collection section.

Again, formative evaluation is intended to measure progress toward goals and to search for problems in the implementation of the center. The key to understanding formative evaluation is recognizing that it is the study of the center while in progress.

SUMMATIVE EVALUATION

Summative (also called *retroactive* or *outcome*) evaluation determines whether the goals have been met. It produces an overview of strengths and weaknesses that is the springboard for beginning the improvement process. It is conducted after results have been measured (therefore after the formative evaluation).

The summative evaluation should not only be concerned with whether the goals were achieved but also whether the goals were worth achieving. The Tennessee State Department of Education (1990) added: "Not only does it provide information on what needs to be added or deleted, what gets the most use and where to make improvements, but it also helps others in the support network to stay informed. Evaluation reports should be sent to all individuals involved in the Career Center." Similar to the various methods of data collection described in this chapter, summative evaluation might take the form of assessments, follow-up studies, interviews, observations, career portfolios, or some blend of these.

The purpose of summative evaluation is to certify program utility (Worthen and Sanders 1987). It is intended to appeal to potential consumers and/or funding agencies. Summative evaluation is often conducted by an external evaluator, attempts to "convince" the audience, is done with limited frequency, and is usually large in scale.

SUMMARY

Understanding your career center's audience is critical to successful continuous planning and improvement. The four key steps in evaluating and meeting the needs of center users are

1. *Needs assessment.* This includes identifying community and environment issues and understanding the needs of individual users.
2. *Program planning.* This should begin with a general mission statement and evolve into outlining expected outcomes and the measurement of outcomes.
3. *Formative evaluation.* This is also called *process* or *proactive evaluation* because it assesses the ongoing processes of development and implementation.
4. *Summative evaluation.* This is also called *retroactive* or *outcome evaluation* because it assesses the outcome of the planning and development activities.

To reinforce this notion of planning and evaluation as a continuous process, the chapters focusing on specific target audiences also discuss specific planning, assessment, and evaluation strategies. The intention is to encourage revisiting these issues periodically and within the context of the career center program.

CHAPTER 3

Developing Your Facilities

by Donald A. Schutt Jr.

Here are a number of questions that need to be answered as facilities are developed. The first is whether there is space already existing that has been identified as career center space. If the answer is yes, that space may guide the development process. If the answer is no, there may be more opportunities for creativity and design. This chapter focuses on the physical design of a career center, including consideration of equipment and technology needs.

LOCATION

The physical location of the center is likely to impact use. The following suggestions should help to ensure that the location of your center produces a positive impact.

1. Be near the main flow of traffic. This means different things to different centers. One example from Waukesha, Wisconsin (near Milwaukee), came when the staff was developing a Workforce Development Center. They did not have a site selected or building space identified, so their criteria for the location selection process included

- Near Interstate 94 [a major highway in the area] transportation corridor on existing or logical extension of public transportation.
- Proximity to Waukesha and Milwaukee (population center) labor force.
- "Neutral" site outside major city locations.
- Site providing visibility and positive image.

(Workforce Development Center 1997)

Further, their evaluative criteria in the site selection process included items like "size of parcel," "land/topography," "soil conditions," "existing vegetation," and "architectural controls." While their specific needs might be different from those of other centers, the critical point is a location near the main flow of traffic. The Workforce Development Center found a site that met all their criteria on the Waukesha County Technical College grounds. The goal was to develop a community career center that combined community services with a career center. They achieved their goal. The building currently integrates the services of nine agencies and 110 employees and provides career services in about one-third of the building and career-related services in the remaining two-thirds.

In schools the "main flow of traffic" area might translate to the main floor or near the cafeteria. Carefully choosing a physical location in your community, organization, or school provides both visibility for the center and easy entry for the users. If the goal is to have the center put to use, it is vital that it not be too far off the beaten path.

2. Be near the building entrance and close to parking. This also may differ depending on whether users will already be located in the building or whether they will need to find parking to visit. Recognize that new users may know how to get to your building but may not know how to get to the career center once inside. If the center is located away from the main entrance, be sure to prepare and post proper signage to direct potential users to the center. A negative experience getting to the center might prematurely end a visit.

3. Stay away from high noise levels. This pertains particularly to school or other settings where there is potential for noise from athletic or music events or classes that might intrude on work being done in the career center. This also relates to noise from heating/cooling systems, street traffic, or other interference from the outside environment. If the center is planning on providing individual assessment services, there should at least be a quiet room protected from distracting noise that might reduce the effectiveness of the assessment process.

4. Be near the offices of trained professional counselors or career development facilitators. Since career-related issues often overlap with life issues, it is important to consider how the center will respond when individuals need services or present questions and concerns that the center cannot address. Having counselors available as part of your center staff or in nearby offices is one strategy for alleviating this challenge. Madison East High School in Madison, Wisconsin, located the school counseling offices immediately adjacent to the career center. This offers students an opportunity to have contact with their counselors as they explore, investigate, and plan for their careers. It also creates opportunities for counselors who are working with students to go to the career center and assist them in the career development process.

Choosing a location is an important task. Keep in mind the population that the center intends to service and choose a location that best fits those users' needs. Once a site is chosen, design and layout become the next critical considerations.

DESIGN AND LAYOUT

The design and layout of a center is influenced by responses to the following questions.

1. What types of services does the center plan to offer? The services provided can assist in the design of the layout for a career center. The New Mexico State University Career Center divided the space into seven areas: the Career Resource Room, the Office of Career Planning Coordinator, the computer room, the Office of Placement Coordinator, the Job Opportunity Board, the college catalog collection, and the career center reception area.

2. How accessible is the center for individuals with disabilities? Designing an accessible site is important. Tindall, Gugerty, Thuli, Phelps, and Stoddard (1994) examined the needs of three groups of individuals—those with mobility impairments, those with visual impairments, and those with hearing impairments—relative to planning accessible conferences and meetings. They suggested the following points be considered (here adapted for career center use):

Individuals with Mobility Impairments
- Accessibility of main entrances to the site
- Doorways wide enough to accommodate wheelchairs and three-wheel carts of varying sizes
- Appropriately graded ramping in inaccessible areas (including meeting rooms and lounge areas) and directional signs to nearest accessible entrance
- Wide spaces, corridors, and aisles
- Level surfaces
- Accessible restrooms (including wide doors, unobstructed sinks of appropriate height, large stalls, grab bars, adequate space in which to maneuver a wheelchair, and controls and equipment easily operated from a sitting position)
- Public telephones at accessible height
- Adequate space for wheelchairs in meeting rooms and at tables
- Wheelchair-accessible registration tables
- Electrical outlets, light switches, and closet rods of appropriate height

Individuals with Visual Impairments
- Well-lit areas with adjustable lighting
- Obstacle-free environment (i.e., free of protruding objects that cannot be detected easily)
- Large, tactile directions for equipment, elevators, and restrooms; elevator numbers written in braille or raised print

Individuals with Hearing Impairments
- Rooms equipped with alternative emergency devices such as visual alarms and indicators (i.e., flashing lights on doors, telephones, and fire alarms), volume-controlled phone lines, and close-captioned television
- An available TDD (telecommunication device for the deaf)

The Center for Universal Design (CUD) at North Carolina State University promotes the design of products and environments to be usable by all people, to the greatest extent possible, without the need for adaptation or specialized design. CUD delineated seven principles for Universal Design:

1. Equitable Use: The design is useful and marketable to people with diverse abilities.
2. Flexibility in Use: The design accommodates a wide range of individual preferences and abilities.
3. Simple and Intuitive Use: Use of the design is easy to understand, regardless of the user's experience, knowledge, language skills, or current concentration level.
4. Perceptible Information: The design communicates necessary information effectively to the user, regardless of ambient conditions or the user's sensory abilities.
5. Tolerance for Error: The design minimizes hazards and the adverse consequences of accidental or unintended actions.
6. Low Physical Effort: The design can be used efficiently and comfortably and with a minimum of fatigue.

7. Size and Space for Approach and Use: Appropriate size and space is provided for approach, reach, manipulation, and use regardless of user's body size, posture, or mobility.

(Adapted from: http: www.design.ncsu.edu/cud/about_ud/ uprinciples.htm retrieved on April 22, 2007)

More specific details—from curb ramps to parking zone sizes to sinks—should not be overlooked. There are also a number of Internet sites that provide much greater detail regarding access (and the laws) for individual with disabilities. Check these three sites for more specific details:

- The U.S. Department of Justice (http://www.usdoj. gov/crt/ada/adahom1.htm)
- The U.S. Access Board, also known as the Architectural and Transportation Barriers Compliance Board (http:// www.access-board.gov/adaag/html/adaag.htm)
- Center for University Design at North Carolina State University (http://www.design.ncsu.edu/cud/)

3. How large is the physical size of the print, audio, and video resource collection? Sufficient room needs to be allotted for the size and organization of the collection the center develops. Include space for users to sit and examine the materials. Local professionals who have expertise in these areas (librarians, for example) may be very useful as resources regarding the space and equipment necessary to adequately design the center.

4. How many people does the center intend to serve at any one time? One of the biggest challenges is developing a center with the capacity to serve large numbers. Once the center has identified the population it intends to serve, develop a plan for delivering services that includes a variety of methods, some of which may be off-site.

Search for alternate methods of delivering services that do not require the physical presence of the user (for example, an Internet site that provides much of the career-related support needed by users).

In Florida a unique partnership between the schools in two counties (Volusia and Flagler), a community college, and the local Workforce Development Boards resulted in the Career Connection Coach. The Career Connection Coach is a mobile career resource center equipped with the latest multi media technology that provides individual career assessment, exploration, and planning opportunities.

While the coach serves a comparatively small number of students at any one time, it can serve a larger geographic area than any stationary center. Conveniently, it can go to the students rather than the students having to go to it. The area inside the coach has been carefully developed to provide computer workstations, and also meeting/noncomputer work space. This is a very creative approach to addressing the needs of the users where they live.

5. What different methods of delivery are anticipated? Is there a need for classrooms? Space for workshops or other meetings? The method of delivering career information and counseling is coupled with the identified user population characteristics, the amount of space available, the staff strengths, and the goals of the center. It might also be valuable to consider providing center users with experiential workstations to experiment with tasks associated with different occupations.

Also consider the different learning styles that users bring to the center. For some users, written information may be enough, while others might seek workshops and interactive classes to gather the information or assistance they need. Carefully consider the types of services the center plans to offer prior to designing the center because it is difficult to create classroom space once the layout has been completed.

6. How much space is necessary to accommodate people and the technology (including computers, overhead projector, audio and video) used? Provide space for users' computer workstations. Space on either side of a workstation should be free so that several users can view the computer at one time. In some cases this might also be a place for students and their parents to investigate and explore career information on the Internet, or for an adult to work on her or his resume.

If the center plans on offering workshops or classes, be sure to include adequate room space and rooms that are accessible. Some centers use recessed screens for overheads or computer projectors that can transform a career center into a meeting room. Also consider using a lighting system with a dimmer switch to allow for image projection while providing enough light for workshop participants to write notes.

Again, if assessment is taking place at a center that also uses a lot of audio or video, consider designing the center in such a way that the two activities can occur at the same time. If that is not possible, note that as a challenge when it comes to scheduling activities in the center.

7. What can be done to make the career center aesthetically appealing and welcoming? Potential users must see the career center as a friendly environment in which they are free to browse and work at their own pace. Such an environment can be created by some simple decorating maneuvers. If you are starting from scratch or have the opportunity to redecorate existing facilities, choose paint and carpeting in warm, inviting colors. Lighting must be appropriate for reading and other tasks, but it should not be overbright or harsh. You might consider powerful individual reading lamps to complement softer overhead lighting. Furniture—especially chairs—should be comfortable and present a well-coordinated look. Every career center can arrange colorful, orderly displays of handouts, books, and other materials. Green plants, inexpensive and easy to care for, are good ways to combat even the most unwelcoming or utilitarian settings.

Finally, plan ahead for growth and expansion. Try to anticipate the needs of the community one year from now, even five years from now. Using the labor market information, will the community experience new growth or will many of the currently employed citizens lose their jobs? Develop a layout that can deal with short-term capacity overload, and prepare for long-term growth.

EQUIPMENT

Choosing the right equipment may depend on the type of center developed. Barbieri (1991) identified three different levels of career resource centers.

The first level center, or *core center,* offers basic reference material and a designated location for interactions between users and center staff or representatives from the community. Where space is at a premium, particularly in an academic setting, a core center can easily be established in a corner of an existing library. A core center must include tables, chairs, bookshelves, job board, and check-out facilities. It must also have a basic selection of books and materials from each of the three categories outlined in Chapter 4, which is to say assessment tools, career and labor market information, and strategy-based references. Where reference materials are limited, the center can provide lists of resources that are available in nearby public libraries or elsewhere.

The second level center, or *expanded core center,* includes everything in the core center plus more resources connected to high technology. A VCR with a monitor is a simple and useful addition, as is a fax machine. A computer with a printer, CD-ROM drive, and Internet access is becoming a necessity and should be added to your center at this stage. However, the most complete and well-established career resources are still print-based, so take care to ensure that your expanded core center contains an expanded print section as well.

Barbieri (1991) described the third level as the *comprehensive center.* At this level, a center should facilitate individual and group activities, as well as provide career counseling staff for advice and technical support. It goes without saying that comprehensive centers should also update and expand their collections of print and electronic media.

Specific items, particularly reference materials, will differ among academic and adult career centers, but all centers should make provision for the entire career development process. Most career centers possess items from the following list. Your own checklist or shopping list will, of course, be determined by your budget and the needs assessment explored in Chapter 2.

- bookshelves
- bulletin boards
- chairs
- computers and monitors
- computer printers
- computer projector
- computer scanners
- computer server
- computer tables
- copy machine
- desks
- disk storage facility
- display shelves
- fax machine
- file cabinets
- job board
- modem
- monitor
- overhead projector and screen
- portable cart for vcr & monitor
- registration/checkout station
- room dividers
- tables

- telephone(s)
- typewriter
- typing table
- VCR & monitor
- workstations

Consider carefully the medium most appropriate for the primary population served by the center. While there may be many options when it comes to videos, are they the most effective medium for the center's target audience? Longer videos in particular might not hold the audience's attention when compared to the fast connections of the Internet. Talk with other centers, or with organizations and schools that presently work with the target audience before purchasing materials that may be underutilized.

TECHNOLOGY

One of the most costly and challenging investments that career centers make is their computer system. To address the issue of rapid technological changes, it is important to develop a plan for how computer technology can assist users with the career development process. From that plan, decisions can be made regarding hardware and software. Often, technology plans "simply itemize what computers and software will be purchased, what will be networked and where the computers will be located. They seldom address how the technology will be used or how teachers [and staff] are to be trained" (Golden 1997).

Making decisions about technology has only become more complex over time, with many options and opportunities available. Often technology choices are decided on limited information and by a small number of decision makers. When choosing a new technology, collaboration between the administrators, service and program staff, and the end users should be integrated throughout the process. The Instructional Communications System (ICS) at the University of Wisconsin-Extension (2006) suggested that any technology investment should be preceded by a needs analysis to determine a good fit between intentions and effective delivery. In addition, ICS offered the following list of questions to determine which technology is needed:

- How will the technology(ies) improve learning within the organization?
- Is the type of technology needed that will enable instructors and learners to see each other?
- Is the type of technology needed that will require specific fixed site equipment?
- Will a special room or area be needed to use the technology?
- Can the technology be supported by current staff?
- Are there other products or services that are needed to make the technology work?
- Can this technology be easily combined with other technology(ies)?
- How difficult will it be to train instructors and learners to use the technology? (http://www.uwex.edu/ics/design/seltech.htm retrieved on April 22, 2007)

Once the needs assessment has been completed, the career center is ready to move into the planning stage.

Here are some guidelines for developing the plan (adapted from Golden 1997).

- List the hardware, software, and infrastructure that will be required and show how it all works together and with existing technologies.
- Explain how the technology will be integrated with other services, into school curricula, and into local educational agencies, and how it will enhance learning.
- Describe how the career center will ensure ongoing, sustained professional development for staff and users.

- Show which supporting resources—such as services, software, and print resources—will be acquired to ensure successful and effective use of technologies.
- Project the total cost of the technology to be acquired and related expenses needed to implement such a plan.
- Describe how the career center will involve the community in the plan's development.
- Describe a process for the ongoing evaluation, including how technology will affect career development and progress toward meeting center and user goals.

Staff often struggle with what equipment to purchase. Consult qualified and knowledgeable resources in management information systems, instructional technology, LAN managers, or computer technicians when developing the plan. A sample configuration for a computer (a PC in this case) might look like this:

- Pentium 4, 2.8GHz
- NTFS File System
- Memory: 1.0GB, Non-ECC, 533MHz (with more than one slot for expansion)
- USB Keyboard and USB 2-Button Optical Mouse with Scroll
- 80GB SATA 3.0Gb/s, Hard Drive
- 3.5 inch, 1.44 MB, Floppy
- 48X32 CDRW/DVD Combo
- USB 2.0 slots (minimum four)
- Integrated Audio Card and inexpensive speakers
- Support for DirectX 9 graphics
- Internet access
- Minimally 128 MB graphics memory
- Windows XP Professional or Windows Vista Business (note: be sure to check the specific hardware requirements for each operating system prior to making purchase)
- 19-Inch Flat Panel Monitor

This configuration is based on the Windows platform; for other platforms see: http://support.webex.com/support/system-requirements. html. Also important in the configuration are the needs of the user. Microsoft has an excellent resource online (http://www.microsoft. com/technet/prodtechnol/windows2000pro/evaluate/featfunc/ makingco.mspx, retrieved on April 22, 2007) that identified accessibility issues in three different categories:

1. Visual impairments run the gamut from mild nearsightedness to blindness, and they affect users' ability to see information onscreen. Users with visual impairments need high-contrast color schemes, enlarged fonts, and alternative output, including text-to-speech translators and Braille.
2. Users with hearing impairments, ranging from slight hearing loss to deafness, require visual instead of audible cues. A program might flash its title bar when an error occurs, for example, instead of beeping. In general, hearing impairments don't prevent people from using computers but assistive technology gives them a better experience.
3. For people with physical impairments, moving or controlling movements is difficult. These users have difficult using a mouse or keyboard. For example, they might bounce a key, which programs interpret as pressing the key twice, or they have trouble controlling the mouse pointer, making it hard to drag objects. Physical impairments range from unsteady hands to people using mouthsticks.

The site also provided an extensive set of solutions to user accessibility issues. While this sample computer configuration might seem extravagant, it demonstrates the need to contemplate future needs when making computer-related purchases. Keep in mind that purchases today may have to last for many years and must be easy to upgrade and expand with the changes in technology.

Once the computers are in place, connecting to the Internet should be a consideration. Naturally, there are additional costs involved, most obviously for the external connection (the wide area networks connecting schools to each other and to the Internet) and the internal connection (local area networks that link computers within a given organization). While most career centers have computers that are connected to a network housed on a server though a series of wiring and cables, there is increasing interest in adding wireless networks. Wireless networks offer greater mobility, provide opportunities for career center users to bring in personal computers to access the Internet, and save the cost and trouble of adding additional wiring to existing walls. The Wi-Fi Alliance, comprised of over 250 members from several industries, was created to "form a global, non-profit organization with the goal of driving the adoption of a single worldwide-accepted standard for high-speed wireless local area networking" (http://www.wi-fi.org/about_overview. php). The Wi-Fi Alliance recommended a five-step process for setting up a wireless network that progressed from planning to equipment selection to set up to adding the network connections for desktop computers to security. This process would help to clarify and balance effectiveness with efficiency. One of the best examples is the balance between providing enough coverage (and access points) to meet the needs of existing and future users while at the same time maintaining a strong enough signal to keep the data flowing smoothly and quickly throughout the network.

Computers provide access to information and experiences unheard of in the past, but they come at a price greater than the bottom line on the order form—the costs of training staff and users and of ongoing operational support must be taken into account.

SUMMARY

The physical components of your career center can be just as crucial to its success as the staff and materials inside it. The primary physical considerations are

- *Location.* The center should be near the main flow of traffic, away from noise and other distractions, and close to complementary facilities such as the offices of professional counselors.
- *Layout.* The layout and design must be suited to all the activities offered, accessible for users with a variety of disabilities, and large enough to accommodate all materials and anticipated visitors.
- *Equipment.* This includes everything from basic tables and chairs to optional fax machines and computer scanners.
- *Technology.* Costly but necessary, technological needs must be seriously considered and carefully planned for. Career centers might seek the advice of software and network specialists before committing to technology purchases.

CHAPTER 4

Critical Center Resources

by Donald A. Schutt Jr. and Jane Finkle

Resources help career center users answer the three questions posed earlier: *Who am I? Where am I going?* and *How do I get there?* New resources are appearing on the market at a rapid pace. Most are exceptional in quality, but the consumer needs to clearly identify the needs of the center (as developed in Chapter Two) and then find resources that support the goals. Make a commitment to keep the resources current. This can be done by supplementing time-sensitive materials with alternate resources that are available over the Internet, for example. The many resources critical to a career center can be categorized into three basic areas: assessment tools, career and labor market information, and strategy-based references. Any resources or reference materials provided by a career center should be evaluated for bias and stereotyping. In addition, consideration to the language needs of your center users is also important when making decisions related to obtaining materials, resources, and services.

ASSESSMENT TOOLS

These tools help users learn more about themselves. The tasks that might be achieved with assessment tools include identifying individual strengths and weaknesses, fine tuning goals, determining academic skill levels, and conducting an interest and aptitude inventory. These tools range from formal psychometric instruments to informal resources such as portfolios and career-related games. In addition, they can measure different personality characteristics or areas.

It is vital to identify what it is you wish to find out and then seek an instrument that provides that information. For example, there are inventories that specifically measure aptitude (such as the Armed Services Vocational Aptitude Battery, or ASVAB), those that measure interests (such as the Self-Directed Search, or SDS), and others that measure values (the Temperament and Values Inventory). Kapes, Mastie, and Whitfield (1994a) pointed out that "before deciding to employ psychometric instruments for career assessment there is prerequisite contextual information the user needs to possess. This includes a knowledge of the instruments available for the intended use, access to sources of good information about the available instruments and awareness of the various legal, ethical and social considerations that impact the career assessment process." An example of a resource that can increase knowledge of a broad range of career-related instruments, published by the National Career Development Association, is *A Counselor's Guide to Career Assessment Instruments* (Kapes, Mastie, and Whitfield 1994b).

To select an instrument, Mehrens (1994) recommended using this outline:

1. State your purpose for testing
2. Describe the group that will be tested (e.g., age or grade)
3. Name of test
4. Author(s)
5. Publisher
6. Copyright date(s)
7. Purpose and recommended use as stated in the manual
8. Grade/age levels for which the instrument was constructed

9. Forms: Are equivalent forms available? What evidence is presented on the equivalence of the forms?
10. Format: comment on legibility, attractiveness, and convenience
11. Cost
12. Content of test and types of items
13. Administration and timing requirements
14. Scoring processes available (e.g., machine scoring)
15. Types of derived scores available
16. Types and quality of norms
17. Adequacy of reliability evidence presented in the manual
18. Validity evidence
19. General quality of administrative, interpretive and technical manuals
20. Comments about the instrument by outside reviewers
(Mehrens 1994)

In addition, consider these questions when selecting assessments:

• Is the reading level at the level of the intended users?
• Is the instrument published in languages other than English?
• Are there alternate formats for visually impaired users?
• Are the measures timed (and if so, do the norms also report any differences for users with disabilities who might need additional time)?
• Does your staff have the competence and training needed to ethically administer and interpret the results?

Historically, another source of information on assessments was the National Occupational Information Coordinating Committee (NOICC) and its state counterparts, the State Occupational Information Coordinating Committees (SOICCs). "The originating legislation for both NOICC and the SOICCs was Section 161 of the Education Amendments of 1976 (Committee on Education and Labor, PL 94-142). This legislation charged the committees to develop and implement a standardized occupational information system to serve the needs of vocational education and employment and training programs" (Flanders, 1988). Funding for these systems was not included in the federal budget for the year starting in July 2007 in the same way as it had been in the past. There may still be SOICCs operating in your state; your state department of labor may have the most current information. Typically, SOICCs work in three areas: career development, information delivery, and training and technical support. In terms of assessment, some SOICCs have developed customized assessment instruments that are integrated into the Career Information Delivery System (CIDS) for the state. If your SOICC has not developed instruments, they may be able to refer career centers to the appropriate organization or resources in your area. Generally, the various SOICCs offer both print and electronic resources.

Examples of frequently used career-related computer software programs and Internet resources that offer a combination of assessment tools with career and labor market data include

- Bridges (http://bridges.com)
- CareerExplorer (JIST Works, 8902 Otis Avenue, Indianapolis, IN 46216-1033, http://www.jist.com)
- COIN Career Guidance System (COIN Educational Products, 3361 Executive Parkway, Suite 302, Toledo, OH 43606, http://www.coin3.com)
- Discover (ACT, Educational Services Division, P.O. Box 168, Iowa City, IA 52243-0168, http://www.act.org/discover/)
- FOCUS (for high school students) (http://www.focuscareer.com/)
- Magellan (Valpar International Corp., P.O. Box 5767, Tucson, AZ 85703-5797, http://www.valparint,com/magellan.htm)
- SIGI³ (Valpar International, PO Box 5767, Tuscon, AZ, 85703, http://www.sige3.org)

There are also many print resources that have been used as informal assessments assisting in the career development process, including

- Center on Education and Work, University of Wisconsin-Madison. 1997. *STW Self-assessment Checklist.* Madison, WI: Center on Education and Work, University of Wisconsin-Madison.
- Hood, A. B., and Johnson, R. W. 2006. *Assessment in Counseling: A Guide to the Use of Psychological Assessment Procedures.* 4th ed. Alexandria, VA.: American Counseling Association.
- Vernon, A. 2004. *Developmental Assessment and Intervention with Children and Adolescents.* 2d. ed. Alexandria, VA.: American Counseling Association.
- *What Color Is Your Parachute?* 2006. Berkeley, Calif.: Ten Speed Press.
- Zunker, V. G. 2005. *Using Assessment Results for Career Development.* 7th ed. Belmont, Calif.: Wadsworth Publishing.

Regardless of the assessment instrument used, it is important to establish why and how the instrument was selected; which staff has the training necessary to administer, score, and interpret the instrument; and how the results will be communicated to the client.

CAREER AND LABOR MARKET INFORMATION

Complete, accurate, and timely information is critical as individuals make career decisions and form career plans. Career and labor market information responds to the question, *Where am I going?* As DeYoung (1998) noted, "career centers typically unify many functions such as intake, assessment, case management, employer services, and inter-agency planning." Career and labor market information can assist center users by offering opportunities for "career awareness, job and career counseling, training and educational referrals, job search assistance, literacy services, and occupational training." Career center users should be able to locate and use occupational information in making career decisions and developing their career plans. The occupational data that should be available to all users includes

- duties and nature of work,
- work setting and conditions,
- preparation required,
- special requirements or considerations (bonafide physical requirements, licenses, certifications, personal criteria, social or psychological factors, etc.),
- methods of entry,
- earnings and other benefits,
- usual advancement possibilities,
- employment outlook,
- opportunities for experience and exploration,
- related occupations, and
- sources of additional information.

(National Career Development Association 1994)

Career (or occupational) information is valuable to the user who is looking for information on employment trends, qualifications of employment, job descriptions related to a variety of occupations, and specific career or job openings. "It also consists of personal/ social, educational and occupational information emphasizing individual characteristics, attributes, skills, knowledge, interests, values and aptitudes. This information is generally used by career decision makers and career guidance professionals to discover and explore occupational opportunities, related educational programs of study and training, the institutions that offer the programs, and other related information" (Ettinger 1996b). Career information assists users in picturing the work tasks and work environment by providing occupational descriptions. An example is a book or video focused on career biographies. Typically, it supplements the individual's perceptions of an occupation with the realities and allows for comparisons between occupations by providing the same data for each occupation or job. It can also be used to identify how one enters or advances in an occupational area, and the education/training necessary for success.

Labor market information is helpful to individuals who are looking for or exploring employment in a specific field or are interested in general job opportunities in a given geographic area. It is "data about workers, jobs, industries and employers including employment, demographic and economic data. It is generally used by administrators, planners, information analysts, policy makers, employers, and job seekers" (Ettinger 1996b). By reviewing the trends and outlooks for occupations, users can challenge misconceptions regarding areas where occupations are growing or shrinking. Labor market information also contributes to the picture users have of occupations as the industry or business data offers an idea of what is produced in any given industry.

Together, career and labor market information are used to gather background data regarding occupations, choose occupations, change work settings, or search for opportunities in specific geographic areas. In terms of computer software, the programs listed earlier also provide occupational and/or career information. A short list of print reference tools that should be considered include:

- Dunbar, R. E. 1998. *Guide to Military Careers*. Danbury, Conn.: Franklin Watts.
- *Encyclopedia of Careers and Vocational Guidance*. 2007. 14th ed. New York: Ferguson.
- Maze, M., and Mayall, D. 1995. *The Enhanced Guide for Occupational Exploration*. 2d. ed. Indianapolis, Ind: JIST Works.
- O*NET Dictionary of Occupational Titles http//.www.dictionary-occupationaltitles.net.
- U.S. Census Bureau. 2002. North American Industry Classification System (NAICS) http://www.census.gov/epcd/www/naics.html.

- U.S. Department of Defense. 2001. *America's Top Military Careers: The Official Guide to Occupations in the Armed Forces.* 3d ed. Indianapolis, Ind.: JIST Publishing.
- U.S. Department of Labor and Bureau of Labor Statistics. 2006. *Occupational Outlook Handbook 2006-07 Edition.* http://stats.bls.gov/oco/home.htm.

In addition to the tools listed in the previous section, there are other Internet and computer software programs that provide career and labor market information. These are just a few examples:

- *America's Career Infonet*: http://www.acinet.org
- *Career & College QUEST* (Peterson's, 2000 Lenox Drive, P.O. Box 67005, Lawrenceville, NJ 08648, http://www.petersons.com)
- *Career Information System* (National Career Information System, 1244 University of Oregon, Eugene, OR 97403-1244)
- *Electronic Enhanced Dictionary of Occupational Titles* (JIST Works, 8902 Otis Avenue, Indianapolis, IN 46216-1033, http://www.jist.com)
- *Ferguson's Career Guidance Center* (Ferguson, 132 W. 31 St, New York, NY, 10001, http://www.factsonfile.com)
- *The O*NET Dictionary of Occupational Titles* (JIST Works, 8902 Otis Avenue, Indianapolis, IN 46216-1033, http://www.jist.com)
- *Peterson's Graduate Database (GradSearch)* (Peterson's, 202 Carnegie Center, P.O. Box 67005, Princeton, NJ 08648, http://www.petersons.com)

In addition to the resources mentioned above, many publishing companies and distributors currently publish quality career-related materials. New materials are appearing constantly. Even though many of the materials that the career center purchases will likely come from for-profit publishers and educational material distributors, do not overlook alternate suppliers, including the American Vocational Association; the National Career Development Association; the American School Counselor Association; the Department of Labor; the military; community surveys; Chambers of Commerce; labor unions; newspapers and magazines for time-sensitive information; corporations; federal, state, and local government printing offices; other professional and trade organizations; and colleges and universities.

There are also a number of resources that provide national data that can be accessed via the Internet. One is the Bureau of Labor Statistics (BLS) (http://bls.gov), the national statistical agency responsible for collecting, processing, analyzing, and disseminating statistical data to the public. As their home page states, "BLS data must satisfy a number of criteria, including relevance to current social and economic issues, timeliness in reflecting today's rapidly changing economic conditions, accuracy and consistently high statistical quality, and impartiality in both subject matter and presentation." The BLS has developed user friendly pages geared to draw in interest from a number of different populations.

One site available at the national level is the O*NET (http://www.online.onetcenter.org). This is the Occupational Information Network, designed to replace the *Dictionary of Occupational Titles (DOT)*. The O*NET database, according to its Web site is "the nation's primary source of occupation information" The actual database structures information into six categories: worker requirements, experience requirements, occupational requirements, occupation specifics, occupation characteristics, and worker characteristics. Additional Internet sites that might be of interest include FedStats (http://www. fedstats.gov/), the U.S. Census Bureau (http://www.census. gov/), and the Bureau of Economic Analysis (http://www.bea. gov/).

STRATEGY-BASED REFERENCES

These resources assist the career center user with the development of resumes (paper and electronic formats), provide tips on interviewing, strategies for approaching businesses, and methods for interview follow-up. Topics include

- developing workplace skills,
- positive work habits,
- test preparation materials (SAT, ACT, ASVAB, etc.),
- scholarship and financial aid information,
- college materials,
- job seeking materials,
- cover letters,
- resume writing,
- interviewing,
- getting a job and keeping it,
- recruitment literature, and
- military materials.

Some of these resources might include a combination of self-assessment, career and labor market information, and strategy-based references. Sources in this category include

- Farr, J. M. 2001. *Getting the Job You Really Want.* 4th. ed. Indianapolis, Ind.: JIST Works.
- Figler, Howard E. 1999. *The Complete Job-Search Handbook: Everything You Need to Know to Get the Job You Really Want.* New York: Henry Holt and Company.
- Jandt, F. E., and Nemnich, M. B. 1997. *Using the Internet and the World Wide Web in Your Job Search.* 2d. ed. Indianapolis, Ind.: JIST Works.
- Krannich, C., and Krannich, R. L. 2005. *Interview for Success.* 8th ed. Manassas, V.: Impact.
- Ludden, L. 2002. *Job Savvy: How to Be a Success at Work.* 3d ed. Indianapolis, Ind.: JIST Works.

- Gabler, L. 2000. *Career Exploration on the Internet.* New York: Ferguson.
- Weddle, P. D. 1994. *Electronic Resumes for the New Job Market.* Manassas, V.: Impact.

Strategy-Based References Utilizing the Internet
- Career Decision-Making Tool from America's Career Resource Network (ACRN) http://www.acrnetwork.org/decision.htm
- College Grad : http://www.collegegrad.com
- The Rileyguide: http://www.rileyguide.com
- U.S. Department of Labor 21st Century Workforce Office http://www.dol.gov/21cw/resources.htm
- Wetfeet: http://www.wetfeet.com

Strategy-Based for Specific Audiences
Midlifers
- Walker, Jean Erickson. *The Age Advantage: Making the Most of Your Midlife Career Transition.* New York: Berkley Books. 2000.
- Leider, R. J., & Shapiro, D. A. *Repacking Your Bags: Lighten Your Load for the Rest of Your Life.* San Francisco: Berrett-Koehler Publishers, Inc. 2002.

Minorities
- Friskopp, Annette and Sharon Silverstein, *Straight Jobs, Gay Lives,* 1995, oarsuooabtm N,J,: Scribner.
- Anderson, Sandy, *Women in Career & Life Transitions,* 1999, Indianapolis, Ind.: JIST Works.
- Limited English Proficient individuals http://www.lep.gov/

Disabilities
- Ryan, Daniel J., Ph.D., *Job Search Handbook for People with Disabilities,* 2d. ed. 2004, Indianapolis, Ind.: JIST Works.

EVALUATING MATERIALS

This section considers strategies for evaluating all materials for bias and stereotyping, and then brief, specific evaluations for career-related print, video, and software. The last three sections draw on the National Career Development Association (1994) guidelines for reviewing media. Printed guidelines and evaluation forms are available from the NCDA online at http://ncda.org/ or at 305 North Beech Circle, Broken Arrow, OK 74012, 866-367-6232.

Bias and Stereotyping

It is important to preview all materials and resources before purchasing them for your career center. Many companies allow potential buyers to review their materials before purchasing. This gives you the opportunity to see if the name of the material and the contents are aligned. Careful screening of print, video, and software materials is necessary in order to expand clients' horizons with respect to job opportunities, to help career center users anticipate and deal with bias and discrimination on the job, and to provide them with information on equal employment opportunities. It is critical to help all career center participants understand, think about, and prepare for a future characterized by change and diversity, especially in female and male life roles, relationships, and careers.

There are several general guidelines that can help you with the evaluation of bias in career planning materials. The questions that follow apply equally to print and nonprint materials, in terms of the language, graphics, and the visual representations used. If you answer "no" to any of the questions below, bias, discrimination, and/or stereotyping may be present. It then becomes necessary to further analyze and review the materials, replacing them if necessary. If replacement is not an option, consider developing reference or supplemental material and discuss it with the user.

The following questions can be used as guidelines for rooting out bias in your career center resources:

1. Are occupations shown as open to all individuals regardless of race, sex, religion, creed, parental or marital status, sexual orientation, or physical, mental, emotional, and learning disability?

2. Are gender-free terms used in general (*people* or *humankind* instead of *man* or *mankind*)?

3. Are gender-free titles used to describe occupations (*firefighter* instead of *fireman, postal carrier* instead of *mailman*)?

4. Do females and males appear in approximately the same number?

5. Are males and females depicted in occupations currently dominated by the opposite sex (or are men shown in traditionally masculine careers and/or women in traditionally feminine careers)?

6. Are males and females portrayed in both active and passive roles in approximately the same number (or are men shown more often in active postures with women predominantly depicted as helpers, watching or sitting)?

7. Are various races and ethnic groups represented throughout the resource in a balanced fashion?

8. If references are made to family responsibilities, are the responsibilities shared between the sexes (or is a woman's responsibility to raise a family while a man's responsibility is to be the economic provider)?

9. Are minority and nonminority, males and females, pictured equally in varied levels of occupational status and responsibility?

10. Do illustrations of people include a variety of body types and evidence of handicaps?

11. Is written reference made to physical appearance only when there is a genuine need for it?

12. After reviewing the material, do you come away with a sense that career opportunities are not limited by gender, race, or handicaps?

(Adapted from National Organization for Women 1972)

One strategy for preparing staff to confront issues of bias is to review select materials as a group, with each staff member using the guidelines, and then discussing the results together. In this way you provide a format for training staff in expectations regarding acceptable and unacceptable materials while increasing awareness beyond the confines of the media.

Using the questions above as guidelines will help all staff in the career center

- develop awareness about screening resources before sharing them with the general public;
- teach everyone to analyze the information they are receiving;
- help users become aware of the ways that idioms, expressions, and gender-biased language are used to discriminate; and
- provide the viewer with an opportunity to modify language or illustrations that appear biased.

Another method for ensuring that materials are evaluated to avoid stereotyping and bias is to always have a trained "career advocate" on staff. This individual provides a critical eye and can teach others to look for discriminatory information.

Career and Occupational Information Literature
The key to evaluating printed career and occupational literature information is ensuring that specific kinds of information are made explicit in the text. At a basic level, you should evaluate all literature by date of publication (is it still current?), credits and sources listed (are they unbiased and trustworthy?), format and vocabulary (are they appropriate and useful to the target audience?). The NCDA guidelines also say that occupational information should be evaluated on its inclusion of

1. duties and nature of the work,
2. work setting and conditions,
3. preparation required,

4. special requirements or considerations (including licensing requirements and bonafide physical requirements),
5. methods of entry,
6. earnings and other benefits,
7. usual advancement possibilities,
8. employment outlook,
9. opportunities for experience and exploration,
10. related occupations, and
11. sources of additional information.

Video Career Media

The NCDA guidelines for video career media deals with the objectives, concepts, and information portrayed in the video and the impact on the audience. In addition, they focus on both the content and the process. The guidelines include

1. early presentation of intent (purpose of video must be obvious early in the video),
2. integrity of title (must accurately reflect the content or purpose),
3. free from extraneous (noncareer-related) material (content must be organized to fulfill stated objectives),
4. accurate and adequate presentation of concepts and information (must be portrayed and illustrated in a manner appropriate for the intended audience), and
5. simulates transition from passive to active response (must motivate audience toward appropriate behavioral response).

Career Software

The NCDA software guidelines focus on both the description of the software and the evaluation criteria. As to the description of the software, one should determine its objectives, how it is applicable to career development, whom it is appropriate for, and what skills are prerequisite for using the software. The NCDA further suggests that users also consider the following five aspects of a software program as part of their evaluation:

1. Information in the program
2. Career development process
3. User interaction
4. Technical aspects of the software and materials
5. Support services

Identifying Resources to Meet the Language Needs of Your Users

The U.S. Department of Justice suggested the following steps to identify resources for meeting the language needs through the "Let Everyone Participate" Web site (http://www.lep.gov/). These steps are built on the assumption that the organization has determined the language needs of the community being served.

- Differentiate between the many types of language service providers available, and determine which combination is appropriate for your program.
- When selecting services, consider the strengths and limitations of various language service providers.
- Identify bilingual staff.
- Identify situations requiring the services of a professional interpreter or translator.
- Telephonic interpretation services can ensure resources when in-house demand is high or immediate interpretation is needed.
- Work collaboratively with community groups and academic institutions, and train bilingual/multilingual community members, university professors, graduate and law students, and language educators to provide language services on an as-needed basis.
- Factor language assistance costs into your budget and planning process and include interpreter and translator costs

in grant applications and contracts. (Condensed from: From U.S. Department of Justice "Let Everyone Participate" Web site http://www.lep.gov/lepdoc%20chapterl. htm retrieved April 22, 2007)

More detailed information is available at http://www.lep.gov.

ORGANIZING MATERIALS

There are a number of different methods for organizing materials. The one you choose will depend upon your audience, your collection of materials, and the time and staff available to learn and implement the system. In addition to the methods listed here, you may want to create your own or adapt an established method.

- Academic Subject Classification (school subject area)
- Alphabetical
- Ann Roe's Two-Dimensional Occupational Classification Scheme (occupational titles on one level according to worker activities and the other level focusing on job stratification according to level of responsibility)
- Bennet Occupations Filing Plan and Bibliography (based on the field-of-work coding in the Dictionary of Occupational Titles)
- Categories (like self-understanding, university information, state Career Information Delivery Systems, etc.)
- Chronicle Guidance Publication Plan (also use Dictionary of Occupational Titles and arranged under 10 headings and subdivided into occupational fields)
- Dewey Decimal System (used by many libraries)
- Dictionary of Occupational Titles Occupational Titles Classification
- Holland Occupational Organization System (based on his six work environments and six interest areas)

(McDaniels and Gysbers 1992)

There are also models nationally; one example is provided by the recommendations from the Secretary's Commission on Achieving Necessary Skills released in 1992 (http://wdr.doleta.gov/SCANS/). This commission was appointed by the Secretary of Labor in 1990 to determine the skills our young people need to succeed in the world of work. One report released in June 1991, "What Work Requires of Schools: A SCANS Report for America 2000," provided both the foundations and the competencies on which programs could be built. Those same competencies could be used to organize resources in a career center, or to plan a curriculum delivered by a career center in classrooms or community centers. The foundation included three areas: Basic Skills, Thinking Skills, and Personal Qualities. The competencies were divided into: Resources, Interpersonal, Information, Systems, and Technology. The intended application was to incorporate these competencies based on the foundational areas throughout a curriculum as a way of connecting learners with the world of work.

SUMMARY

The three basic types of resources essential to a career center are assessment tools, career and labor market information, and strategy-based resources. Examples include:

Assessment Tools
- Tests measuring aptitudes (ASVAB), interests (SDS), and values (TVI)
- Computer software (CareerExplorer, SIGI Plus)
- Books and other print resources (*What Color Is Your Parachute?*, *Life Work Career Portfolio*)

Career and Labor Market Information
- Computer software (*Career & College QUEST*, *Encyclopedia of Careers and Vocational Guidance*)

- Books and other print resources (*Occupational Outlook Handbook, Dictionary of Occupational Titles*)
- Internet databases (Bureau of Labor Statistics, O*NET Occupational Information Network)

Strategy-Based Resources
- College and other postsecondary education materials
- Scholarship and financial aid information
- Instruments to improve such skills as interviewing and writing resumes

Prior to purchase, all of the above resources should be evaluated for bias and stereotyping. It is also wise to examine materials for such problems as the inclusion of noncareer-related or extraneous information.

Possible methods of organizing the various resources within a career center include alphabetization, color coding, the Dewey Decimal System, and the DOT Occupational Titles Classification.

CHAPTER 5

Personnel, Administration, and Management

by Donald A. Schutt Jr. and George Watson

There are several approaches to managing the career center. A strong organizational structure is necessary to enable the delivery of the program processes. The framework suggested by NOICC (1995) to guide the development of comprehensive career development programs in schools also applies to the development of career centers that provide support for lifelong career development. The five components of the framework are

1. Leadership: A counselor or career development specialist who is supported by a staff dedicated to improving career development opportunities for users.
2. Management: Top-level staff organizing program planning, clarifying staff roles and responsibilities, securing resources, monitoring program delivery, and revising the program.
3. Personnel: Other staff, community resource persons, paraprofessionals, and volunteers who can help serve the wide range of career development needs through direct involvement or linkages with other organizations.
4. Facilities: Adequate space, materials, and equipment that ensure the delivery of career guidance and counseling services.

5. Resources: The funds required to purchase materials, equipment, and other items needed to implement a career guidance and counseling program.

This chapter considers who should be involved in the development (from external advisory groups to staff) and operation of the center, staff training suggestions, and budget considerations.

DEVELOPMENT AND OPERATION

The Advisory Group

Developing a strong advisory group allows the center to connect with and also take advantage of the resources existing in the community. The advisory group should consist of a diverse representation of career center stakeholders who have a strong interest in seeing the center succeed. Find representatives from the following groups:

- business, industry, trade, or union representatives (maybe from the local chamber of commerce or manufacturers association);
- community leaders (someone from the mayor's office, city or county board, local nonprofit leaders, or key religious figures);
- community members (from the population the center intends to serve);
- K-12 representatives (local school-to-work coordinator, school counselors, teachers, principals);
- past users of the career center (or of other career centers in the area);
- postsecondary representatives (community colleges, two-year and four-year college representatives);
- potential users (draw on people representing the target audiences);
- state government representatives (from the State Occupational Information Coordinating Committee office, the

state department of public instruction or education, or the
governor's office); and

- technology experts to guide the development of the career
  center information system.

In addition, if the career center is in a school, consider selecting
parents, teachers, school counselors, and students to participate
in developing and advising the center. The creation and use of an
advisory group helps to develop strong community relations, opens
communication channels, provides additional insights into selection
criteria for program staff and materials, assists in evaluating the
program, and expands the pool of individuals generating marketing
strategies.

As an advisory group is identified and organized, it is important to be very clear about the roles and expectations of the members of the advisory group. More specifically, if the group is to
provide suggestions or recommendations rather than make final
decisions, be certain that the parameters of the decision-making
process are clear. It is also helpful to orient members to the current
career center (especially if they are entering midstream or if some
of the decisions have already been made). Be open to the advice of
the advisory group and avoid responses that appear defensive. If
an advisory group is formed, the center has already accepted that
the individuals in the group have experiences or perspectives that
are important to the success of the center—draw on that information and use it to fully develop the services and programs at the
center.

Once the group is identified and they have accepted the advisory
group appointment, it is useful to provide an orientation to the
program. Conducting a periodic review of the effectiveness of the
advisory committee is also a useful process. As mentioned in previous chapters, the timing of this review should be decided in the
center's continuous planning and improvement process. To gauge
the effectiveness of the advisory committee, career centers should
ask questions such as these:

Does the advisory committee . . .

✔ Represent a cross-section of the community?

✔ Assist in long-range and short-range planning?
- Establish priorities and develop objectives?
- Locate and support funding efforts?
- Coordinate use of community resources?
- Review and assess career center activities and recommend improvements?
- Assist in the center evaluation process?

✔ Communicate improvement information back to its constituents?

✔ Communicate information about the center to the media?
- Through newsletters?
- Through personal communication with constituencies?
- Through press releases?
- Through public meetings?
- Through reports?
- Through television, radio, Internet communications?

✔ Work together effectively?
- Are meetings scheduled when necessary?
- Is attendance recorded?
- Is there a written agenda distributed?
- Are they a sounding board for new ideas?
- Are other opinions sought and heard?
- Are minutes recorded?

Taking time to create and evaluate the advisory group is valuable during program development as well as during program review.

When advisory groups are used to the fullest potential, they can be a central source for the dissemination of information to stakeholders, the community, and potential career center users. In addition, an effective advisory group can assist in the development of the center's mission, vision, and goals as well as providing an "external" perspective in the development of the center's short-term and long-term planning.

Staffing the Center

The process of identifying staff positions is directly connected to the mission and location of the center, space available, funding sources, services offered, and delivery methods. If the career center is in a middle school, the staff may focus more on integrating career development into the school curriculum, so a curriculum specialist might be more valuable than another position. Likewise, if the physical capacity of the center cannot provide enough room for the materials, a large staff might initially be inefficient. These complexities aside, a skeleton career center staff includes

- a manager/coordinator/director,
- professional counselors,
- professional librarians and information specialists,
- technology experts,
- paraprofessionals (might include support staff),
- volunteers,
- students, or
- some combination of these different employees.

The size of the staff and their individual duties will depend in a large part on how the center operates and how much financial support is available for staff. Career center staff face many challenges: "Staff in contemporary career centers not only must perform their own work, but also must coordinate and mobilize the efforts of dozens of partners seeking similar service goals—academic departments, external agencies, student clubs, campus unions, local businesses, other student service departments, government offices, plus others"

(Casella 1990). Each of the staff positions contributes something different to the career center.

Manager/Coordinator/Director

The person in this leadership and management position must have a strong set of convictions, values, beliefs, and ethics that align with the organization's values and beliefs about career development, coupled with a strong understanding of the field of career development, as well as the components that are critical to developing and supporting comprehensive career development programs, and insights into successful management processes. It is also the responsibility for a manager/coordinator/director to create a workplace climate where individuals thrive and the organization succeeds. Experience writing grants or soliciting funding would be additional desirable skills. Lastly, the manager should be competent in using technology, or at least have enough understanding of technology and systems to manage the use and future needs of technology in the career center.

The tasks of a manager/coordinator/director include: supervising staff, managing the day-to-day operations, searching for financial resources (when needed), developing collaborative partnerships with other organizations including schools and business/industry, and directing the continuous planning and improvement process guided by the mission and vision of the center. Here is a detailed sample job description for the Director of the Career Resource and Assessment Center at community college:

Title of Position
Director of the Career Resource and Assessment Center (CRAC)

Major Job Responsibilities
1. Directly responsible to the Dean of Student Services
2. Responsible for the organization and administration of the CRAC including effectively managing the staff, processes, and functions of the center

3. Administration and/or supervision of the center's testing services

Essential Functions

1. Supervising and/or conducting career counseling and test interpretations for individuals and small groups
2. Providing career consultation and referral services
3. Providing in-service, training, and supervision of CRAC personnel
4. Previewing, evaluating, and purchasing career and testing materials
5. Maintaining a familiarity with test manuals, booklets, procedures, and instructions of major tests and surveys administered by the CRAC
6. Developing and maintaining career files and library
7. Providing/displaying and disseminating information related to career/occupational and social/personal development
8. Revising, updating, and whenever necessary developing operational materials
9. Facilitating and/or conducting career-related seminars, workshops, classroom presentations, etc.
10. Communicating to staff, students, and/or the community information related to services offered, new materials available, upcoming career-related activities, etc.
11. Promote respect and the practice of civility in the workplace
12. Demonstrate a commitment to organizational success
13. Other duties as assigned by the Dean

Requirements

1. Possess at least a master's degree in guidance and counseling, psychology, or equivalent

2. Possess the ability to interpret/analyze, test data of all types (career, personality, aptitude, intelligence, ability, achievement, and placement)
3. Be able to work effectively with people of differing ages, ethnic backgrounds, and gender
4. Be willing to work flexible hours
5. Possess a high energy level along with enthusiasm and a genuine interest in assisting individuals in planning their career development

A disadvantage to having a manager/director is cost. Many centers that originated in a different form, like a library or counseling office, cannot afford a manager/director. Center staff in this situation often divide the managerial tasks among themselves. For most career centers, the most effective approach is to hire a manager/coordinator/director.

Professional Counselor(s)

If the center plans to offer career counseling, it is important that competent, professionally trained and licensed counselors are available to provide the service. How do you differentiate between career advising and career counseling? Rayman described career advising as "brief immediate assistance provided by paraprofessional staff with an emphasis on information giving and receiving. He further characterized individual career counseling as "the establishment of a therapeutic relationship between a professionally trained and skill certified career counselor and a client involving significant psychological content, formal assessment and interpretation, teaching, coaching, and information giving in the context of a one-to-one relationship" (Rayman 1996).

There are three reasons why professional counselors are vital to a career center:

1. It may be that the services the center is preparing to offer fall somewhere between these two areas (of career advising and career counseling), which is why having appropriately trained counselors available to make those decisions are critical to center functioning.
2. It is also not uncommon for individuals seeking career assistance to find that while they want to work on career decision making, other life expectations or situations complicate that opportunity or ability to make the critical decisions. Counselors trained in career development can help individuals identify career-related issues and conflicting life-related issues.
3. Most counselors have received training in the area of career development and assessment.

What criteria can you use to find professional counselors? There is a national organization that connects with many states to identify and certify counselors called the National Board for Certified Counselors (NBCC), located at: http://www.nbcc.org/, by phone at 336-547-0607, or by mail: National Board for Certified Counselors, Inc., Three Terrace Way, Suite D, Greensboro, NC 27403-3660. That Internet site offers an opportunity to get a list of certified counselors in your area. A list of state credentialing boards can be found on the Internet at: http://www.nbcc.org/statesboardsmap.

There is also an area of specialization in counseling certified through the NBCC called the National Counselor Certification (NCC) program. The NCC specialty credential attests to the educational background, knowledge, skills, and competencies of the specialist in the specific area of career counseling. More information can be found about this certification at the NBCC Web site. For National Certified Counselors there are requirements for certification including work experience, course work, professional assessments, and examination. In order to remain certified, these counselors must also participate in continuing education.

As with managers/coordinators/directors, one disadvantage to having professional counselors is salary costs.

Professional Librarian or Information Specialist

Career centers sometimes struggle early on to develop a systematic method for organizing and displaying materials and resources. Professional librarians and information specialists are experts at organizing and cataloging materials. There are three strong reasons for considering professional librarians or information specialists:

1. "Librarians or information specialists are generally aware of the sources of material, how to secure them, classification and filing systems, methods for displaying material, and procedures for the maintenance of the collection" (Brown and Brown 1990).
2. Many have experience organizing materials using technology. This knowledge increases the opportunities for moving the internal career center resources to the Internet and offering access to the career center after conventional office hours.
3. Often they are familiar with strategies for funding resources and may already have a budget for resources.

A strategy for identifying well-trained library staff is to look for graduates from accredited library and information studies masters programs. One source of valuable information in this area is the American Library Association, which maintains a list of accredited master's degree programs online at http://www.ala.org.

One drawback is that a librarian's background in career development may be limited, so much of his or her time would be focused on the organizational tasks. If cost is a factor, this could also be done as a short-term appointment to start up the center's materials; the librarian may then return periodically as a consultant.

Technology Experts

The need for staff with expertise in technology-related areas is easy to understand. One of the challenges that can occur is hiring staff with more than one area of expertise (like an information specialist who is also a Webmaster). The challenge becomes balancing immediate duties with the center's long-term goals. The other challenge is keeping a computer-savvy counselor current with new and increasingly fast changes in technology while also allowing him or her to assist users in career decisions.

As the center approaches hiring technology experts, consider which areas are most important. Following are a few questions to ponder:

- Who will troubleshoot the computer problems on the computers the center currently owns?
- Who will load the career-related software?
- Who will train the staff and users on the software?
- Are the computers networked? Who will manage that network?
- Will your experts need to have technical training in repairing computers?
- Are you planning to have a complicated Internet site that will require continuous updating? Will they need to know how to write HTML language, Common Gateway Interface (CGI) scripts, Java scripts, or place pictures on the site? (If these are unfamiliar terms, it is even more important to have someone skilled in technology on staff.)
- Will you use a content-management Web development tools that offers just-in-time changes to Web pages without the need for advanced Web development skills or staff?

- Is there a need for utilizing project management tools (and perhaps creating a project management team) to effectively manage the development of the content and a site map?
- Will they also be editing the Internet site? Do they have editing skills?
- Will users need to register for activities and can that occur through a Web site?
- Are you planning to keep a database of all users for advertising upcoming events? Do your experts have database experience?
- Will resources be kept in an electronic database?
- Will your experts need to monitor listservs and online discussion rooms related to career development?
- Will they be responsible for an internal e-mail system or intranet?
- Will technology be used to deliver workshops and presentations?

Three main areas that necessitate technology are administering the network or computer system (possibly including the purchase of individual and system hardware), directing the implementation of an Internet site, and managing complex databases. The staff responsible for each area should have practical experience working among all three areas.

This discussion demonstrates the need for advisory group members with expertise in technology. They might even assist in the hiring process for this position. When hiring for technology positions, be sure to have the candidates provide samples of their work. It might be difficult to understand how someone created a unique feature on a Web page, but personally using the feature provides managers with insight into the skill and ability levels of potential staff members.

The challenge related to technology positions is in hiring skilled technology staff and then meeting the salary needs. One alternative can be outsourcing technology demands, although this often costs a great deal more, and centers may have less control over the outcome.

Paraprofessionals and Volunteers

These two groups have been combined as the tasks they undertake are similar in many ways. The daily tasks necessary for operating a career center might include clerical work such as filing, responding to correspondence, answering phones, organizing materials, scheduling appointments for other center staff, or coordinating the logistics for upcoming activities. It might also include orienting new users to the resources and services provided by the center, along with answering questions. It is important that paraprofessionals and volunteers are not asked to take on tasks or roles for which they are not prepared (such as career counseling).

When recruiting paraprofessionals and volunteers, consider past center users, retirees, students, or parents. Once hired, plan orientation and follow-up training sessions for the staff. A formalized program that prepares paraprofessionals is the Career Development Facilitators (CDF) training. "This occupational title designates individuals working in a variety of career development settings. A CDF may serve as a career group facilitator, job search trainer, career resource center coordinator, career coach, career development case manager, intake interviewer, occupational and labor market information resource person, human resource career development coordinator, employment/placement specialist, or workforce development staff person" (http://209.235.208.145/cgi-bin/WebSuite/tcsAssnWebSuite.pl?AssnID=NCDA&DBCode=130285&Action=DisplayTemplate&Page=AWS_NCDA2_cdf_intro_what.html retrieved on April 24, 2007). The CDF program is supported by the National Career Development Association and more information can be obtained at http://www.ncda.org. Provide regular (once every three months if possible) performance feedback to volunteers and paraprofessional staff.

Deciding whom to enlist to complete the tasks in the career centers means finding a balance between cost and success. Often, volunteers are willing to offer shorter periods of available times than are paid staff, who may want half-time or full-time positions. The number of staff may affect the time that managers/coordinators/directors need to spend doing supervision and training. A center that is open five days a week and staffed by volunteers might require eight to 10 individuals to cover the hours of business. A center staffed by paraprofessionals, more costly than volunteers, may only have one or two individuals to cover the same hours. A system combining paraprofessionals and volunteers might be more ideal, providing continuity with lower costs.

Staffing Summary
The composition of the staff is an important component of the center. These recommendations summarize key points to consider:

- Make program development and partnership-building a significant part of a staff person's job description, especially during the start-up phase.
- Once a program or system is up and running, make sure there is someone on staff with enough time to manage partnership relations and to coordinate program improvement and development.
- Hire or designate a program coordinator.
- Make sure specialized programs have enough staff to ensure a low user-staff ratio.
- Accept higher caseloads in programs serving a wider range of users or employers, but do not go beyond the point where the caseloads can be managed effectively.
- Gear caseload size to user characteristics.
- Set staffing patterns to match the size and complexity of the program.

- Make sure staff have a combination of the qualities needed to ensure a successful program.

(Adapted from Hoffinger and Goldberg 1995)

STAFF TRAINING AND DEVELOPMENT

Each of the staff positions listed above carries with it its own education and professional development requirements, but the common thread that connects them all is the need for ongoing training and development as a part of their work time. At a minimum, staff should receive training in the career development process and the role that their career center intends to play. This might include having staff create their own professional development plans using the existing resources in the center. This kind of knowledge of center resources is absolutely necessary for the staff, as are brief refresher courses on the center's policies and procedures.

A moderate level of ongoing staff training might include advanced skills in using the Internet for career development. Additionally, staff should explore the vast array of career development resources now available in many media, even if their own center does not yet own or use them. In terms of content expertise, another example of training at this level might include encouraging paraprofessional staff to become credentialed as a Career Development Facilitator (CDF). Many national organizations—the National Career Development Association, the American School Counselor Association, etc.—and their state affiliates can provide more formalized training opportunities.

Ideally, staff would be trained in customer service and strategic planning as well as the areas mentioned above. As with many other aspects of planning and developing a career center, it is worthwhile to visit and work with other career centers in your area. This not only allows a sharing of ideas, but may also present opportunities to conduct the occasional joint training session.

BUDGET

Preparing a financial plan, including an annual budget is an important task. The financial plan should be prepared in advance of requesting funding and be divided into two categories: one-time costs (or start-up costs) and an operating budget (Brown and Brown 1990; Hoffinger and Goldberg 1995; Workforce Development Center 1995).

Start-up costs include many expenses (e.g. construction, remodeling, site development costs for land or rent, equipment including computer and associated hardware, furniture, legal fees, advertising, travel, opening supplies, etc.) before actual operations begin. It is important to focus on costs and equally important to also look for the desired quality, reputation, and service the center will need. These start-up investments create the foundation on which the future of the center rests. Despite best intentions, actual costs often exceed the estimates, so a common practice is to add a contingency of approximately 20 percent of the total estimate as a cushion for unplanned expenses (http://www.score.org/).

An operating budget should include: salaries and fringe benefits, capital expenses (the cost of replacing, repairing, or purchasing new equipment), costs for materials, advertising costs, office costs (such as postage, utilities, printing costs), professional development costs, and any costs that are imposed by your fiscal agents acting on your behalf.

In addition, a financial plan typically includes at least a one-year profit and loss projection and a cash-flow projection. These projections serve to predict the financial future as well as provide an opportunity to seriously think about the financial operation of the center. The two projections are typically described as:

- The one-year profit and loss projection is considered the heart of the financial plan. It is based on forecasted income from services offered or sales, cost of goods sold, expenses, and desired profit.

Equally or perhaps more important is the cash flow projection. Computing the projected cash flow requires estimating income, start-up costs, operating expenses, and reserves. Estimating cash flow includes the receiving of cash (income) and when payments must be made (expenses). If the profit projection is the heart of your business plan, cash flow is the blood as the center will cease to exist if there is no cash. Knowing the projected cash flow also predicts when borrowing or additional funding may be needed. (http://www.score.org/).

As the center prepares the initial financial plan, consider consulting with Service Corps of Retired Executives, which has offices in most larger cities (or contact them on the Internet at http://www.score.org/). SCORE offers free consultation with retired business professionals and online business counseling. This is a resource that few career centers consider, but it is often relied upon by individuals and groups starting up businesses (which a career center is). Brown and Brown (1990) suggested other resources as the center budget is developed:

- Remodeling: either the maintenance department of the organization or an outside contractor can provide estimates of these costs
- Salaries: check local and institutional salaries
- Furniture and equipment: check catalogs, office supply stores, audiovisual equipment vendors, etc.
- Core collection: contact other centers as well as publisher catalogs (which may also be online) to determine costs
- Other: estimate remaining costs on the basis of other operations within the organization

There is a wide variety of funding sources. Some centers are developed out of school counseling programs, where others have been funded by state job service agencies and still others from school-to-work funding. If the center developers have access to the Internet, these sites might be useful in identifying and preparing grant proposals:

- The Foundation Center Online (information on a variety of topics related to grant finding): http://foundationcenter. org
- The Society of Research Administrators GRANTSWEB (a starting point for accessing grant-related information and resources on the Internet): http://www.srainternational. org/newweb/grantsweb/index.cfm
- Yahoo's grant page: http://www.yahoo.com/education/ Financial_aid/Grants/

If you do not have access to the Internet, contact a local library for assistance. Many of these institutions offer workshops and print information that can guide center developers through the process.

- In general, when dealing with budget and funding issues:
- Recognize program staffing as central to overall program cost.
- Find ways to create efficiencies in staffing and to leverage other resources.
- Consider the cost implications of different organizational and staffing structures.
- Use strategies to lower net additional costs to schools and programs.
- Launch programs with enrollments high enough to justify the necessary investment in staff resources.

(Adapted from Hoffinger and Goldberg 1995)

The preparation and execution of a financial plan (and budget) is crucial to the effective management of every career center. The Internet and your local library can provide leads on possible sources of funding. Regardless of where the funding comes from, career centers must budget for both start-up costs and operating expenses.

SUMMARY

When organizing the management of your career center, it is vital to consider several key components. Developing an advisory group from all sectors of the community can be a valuable first step toward carrying out these key tasks efficiently.

The importance of selecting and maintaining a suitable staff for your center can hardly be overstated. The staff at most career centers might include

- a manager, coordinator, or director;
- professional counselors;
- professional librarians or information specialists;
- technology experts; and/or
- paraprofessionals and volunteers.

Once personnel are in place, it is important to commit to ongoing training and professional development for them to maintain skill levels, and prepare for future organizational needs. Using a detailed financial plan allows you to align resources with the priorities that were identified through the planning process.

The proper planning and execution of a budget is crucial to the effective management of every career center. The Internet and your local library can provide leads on possible sources of funding. Regardless of where you get your funding, you must budget for both start-up costs and operating expenses.

CHAPTER 6

Career Centers in Educational Settings

by Donald A. Schutt Jr. and Pat Schwallie-Giddis

Career centers can serve as a hub in educational institutions around which career development activities occur. While the primary target audience is typically the students, the center should also serve as a resource center for staff, including faculty, student services staff, parents, and counselors. This is often important in elementary schools, middle/junior high schools, and postsecondary institutions. Chapter 1 proposed that career development be considered as a process of answering the three critical questions: *"Who am I?" "Where am I going?,"* and *"How do I get there?"* Schools can prepare students for resolving these lifelong questions by providing developmentally appropriate career-related experiences.

The role of the career center in schools, colleges, and universities is to offer practical and timely information and services to students, to support and increase the instructional capacity of the institution by serving as a resource to the faculty and staff, and to reinforce student progress as they create and implement career plans. This applies to career centers that are located in schools, colleges, and universities as well as those which are located outside of the physical boundaries of the campus but serve student populations.

When considering career development as a develomental progression, it is implied that each develomental stage builds on the previous stage. Therefore, teaching students the process of becoming aware of themselves and the workplace is a necessary preliminary step that leads to the exploration stage. A challenge arises when there is a gap between where schools might expect students to be developmentally and where they really are. It is not uncommon for career development not to be addressed until eighth grade. Essentially this means that the students must compress eight years of developmental career-related learning and skill building into a year or less (around eighth grade). This can result in students not being prepared to make the decisions that they need to make, such as choosing their high school courses. This lack of preparation is complicated by students lacking the personal and workplace information needed to make good decisions, so they might decide to attend a four-year college without regard to future planning. The National Career Development Guidelines can serve as a guide to individual goals at every educational and developmental level. Planning career development programs to meet the competency needs identified in the guidelines is one strategy for ensuring the comprehensive development of individuals.

How can career centers work with institutions at different educational levels? Generally career centers should work to educate students and faculty about their services, and to create programs that support the expansion of career-related activities and experiences into the curriculum. These experiences contribute to students' career development in three essential ways:

- Teaching students the skills necessary to answer the three questions at times when they are developmentally prepared to learn and use the information.
- Assisting faculty in identifying teaching points in existing curricula where the content can be used to teach students the process of connecting course material to the world of work.
- Reinforcing the development of critical career development competency areas by asking students to apply their knowledge and skills to increasingly complex situations.

The following four sections detail additional programming considerations for students at the different educational levels.

ELEMENTARY SCHOOLS

At the elementary level, career counselors should work collaboratively with school faculty to teach students the processes of identifying interests and aptitudes, connecting skills with occupations, connecting learning and school subjects with the world of work, and finally how to use information for planning. More specifically, career centers and elementary schools could provide students with experiences though which students

- realize that understanding one's strengths, values, and preferences is the foundation for education and occupational choices;
- understand that it is possible to achieve personal goals by planning preparation in the present;
- achieve a sense of personal competence to choose and to meet the requirements of educational and occupational alternatives;
- consider the implications of change in one's self, in one's options, and in relation to the need for continuing education throughout life;
- understand the similarities between problem-solving skills and personal decision making skills;
- develop an unbiased, nonstereotyped base of information on which to base later educational and occupational decisions;
- understand that schooling is made up of many opportunities to explore and prepare for life;
- recognize the relationships between academic skills—reading, writing, computation and other subject matter—and how these are used in future educational work options;
- identify occupations in which people work with others, with ideas, or with things;

- consider the relationships between occupation, career, and lifestyle;
- describe the purpose that work serves for different people; and
- consider the importance of effective use of leisure time.

(Adapted from Herr 1976
as cited in Herr and Cramer 1996)

Career centers can expose students to occupations or jobs beyond that which their own life experiences might provide. This is particularly important for students who have life experiences that are limited by constraints like income level. For example a career center might cosponsor an elementary school program such as a "Careers in Uniform Day," where workers from occupations that demand wearing of uniforms come to talk with the students. The career center might organize the structure of the day's events and draw on its community contacts, while the school might provide the physical space, follow-up processing of the event, and lunch for the speakers. Through this event, students could increase their awareness of a variety of occupations that might connect with their interests.

Regardless of the specific methods they use, career centers at the elementary school level should

- educate parents about the career development process so school staffs feel increased support for implementing career-related activities
- work with school staff to increase their understanding of the vital role that they play in the career development process, and help them to see how skills like working with others is an important part of working later in life
- provide educational opportunities for school staff to enhance their understanding of the complexities of the world of work and their connection to it
- cosponsor developmentally appropriate educational events with classroom teachers

- make connections between schools, businesses, industry and post-secondary institutions

Often career development is not understood at the elementary level. For this reason, a few examples of structured interventions by career centers in a few elementary schools may be helpful.

Elementary teachers and career counselors can collaborate to provide a classroom of school-wide activities that introduce students to the world of work. In addition to the Careers in Uniform Day, a specific occupation like journalism might be highlighted with a variety of speakers discussing the many kinds of occupations associated with a newspaper, TV news departments, or publishing company. Also a government day could use the same concept, but with a city manager explaining the many varied departments/jobs needed to run a city effectively. The old idea of a school-wide career fair is also still relevant, even if limited to occupations available in the immediate community.

The counselor can also work with teachers in using career materials both in print and on video or Internet to promote interest in exploring various occupations. Some interesting activities can be arranged for grammar and art activities such as draw and write what your parents do for a job or for recreation, and explain how is money involved in each of these activities. If the counselor works with the classroom teachers many innovative ideas can emerge.

MIDDLE/JUNIOR HIGH SCHOOLS

Career centers can work with middle/junior high school educators to provide experiences for students and for staff. Students at this level need to

- understand that achievement of one's goals in life is related to a positive attitude toward work and learning;
- lean how to use a career planning process by preparing an individual education/career plan for middle school and

how to anticipate changes as a result of personal matura-
tion and social needs;

- develop an awareness of the level of competency in academic areas needed to achieve career goals;
- understand how interests, work values, achievements, and
abilities affect career choice;
- learn that nontraditional occupations offer expended career
opportunities, understand what employers expect of appli-
cants and employees;
- learn about leisure and recreational activities that best fit
personal needs and interests and contribute to personal
satisfaction;
- know the sources of information about available jobs and
how to complete a job application;
- know about training opportunities that will enhance
employment potential;
- develop knowledge of the relationship between school
subjects and future educational and occupational choices
without regard for prejudice, bias, or stereotyping;
- be aware of alternative educational and vocational choices
and the corresponding preparation for them;
- understand the challenges, adjustments, and advantages of
nontraditional occupations;
- be aware of employment trends as they relate to training
programs and employment opportunities; and
- be aware of the factors that impede performance and productivity in the workplace.

   *(From the Pennsylvania Department of Education as
   reported in Herr and Cramer 1996).*

The types of experience that career centers might help develop for
students include job shadowing opportunities, career awareness
fairs, and mentoring relationships with community businesses.

   Career centers can also work with schools to guarantee that
student career assessment results or interest inventory results are

accurately interpreted and the information is used in a manner that is ethical and accurate. Career centers might support the school assessment process with worksheets that connect the assessment to center resources, and then connect the results of that process to student opportunities for greater exploration of the world of work (like information interviews).

Career centers can work collaboratively with school staff to seamlessly infuse career development into the curriculum. This might mean working with teachers to coordinate the content in a number of courses so that students may examine occupations in greater detail or from different perspectives. One example is teaching the *Diary of Anne Frank* at the same time that World War II history is taught. For history class, it might be the ideal time for the class to learn how the composition of the occupational structure shifts in a country during times of war. For English class it might mean identifying possible occupational options for major literary characters based on interest inventories students complete as if they were that character. Timing these two curriculum pieces so they run concurrently is one example of how subtle the infusion of career development might be in curriculum.

Career centers at the middle/junior high school level should

- continues to educate students, school staff, and parents about the career development process;
- publicize the career development resources available in the center to parents and school staff;
- teach students about the many strategies for accessing information and the connections between the information databases;
- work with students to increase skills in the areas of managing information and planning;
- support efforts to get students involved in workplace simulation activities or actual work sites; and
- guide students in the creation of a career development portfolio.

HIGH SCHOOLS

At the high school level, career centers need to help students synthesize the information they have been gathering in the earlier stages of development. Unfortunately, many students are not involved in career development activities and many schools do not infuse career-related experiences into the curriculum. The result is that a number of students reach high school developmentally unprepared to make the decisions they now face.

Herr and Cramer (1996) offered several concerns that need to be discusses as students prepare for the transition from high school to their next destination. While this excerpt addresses primarily career guidance issues, understanding the challenge that high school students face equips a career center with valuable information around which programming can be developed.

1. Because many students will complete their formal education with the senior high school year and thereby terminate their opportunities for the systematic analysis and facilitation of their career development, efforts need to be undertaken to reach all students with career guidance opportunities and to help them develop and implement an individual career plan.

2. The major career guidance emphasis in senior high school needs to be on the specific and comprehensive planning of immediate, intermediate, and future educational and occupational career choices after high school. For many reasons, however, not all senior high school students will be ready for such planning. Many students will need intensive self-awareness or career awareness and exploration activities, either because they did not have such experiences in the junior high school or because they were not ready to profit from them at the time.

3. Owing to the nature of senior high school students and the diversity of their goals, career guidance in senior

high school should include counseling and developmental guidance experiences dealing with study habits, human relations at work, career and educational planning, job search techniques, and job interview skills.

4. Decisions must be made about how career guidance and placement will correspond or differ in the senior high school. Will placement be seen as a process spanning the total senior high school period or an event primarily dealt with in the twelfth grade? Will counselors take sole responsibility for educational and occupational placement or will they share these elements with other persons (such as vocational teachers or employment service counselors) in the school and the community?

5. The senior high school student is confronted with internal pressures to make decisions and to pursue specific types of outcomes. Career guidance can helps students deal effectively with these pressures.

6. The verbal and conceptual skills of high school students are more developed than those of junior high school students, permitting career guidance to proceed along multiple and complex dimensions.

7. Because the major combinations of possibilities following high school are reasonably clear—college, other postsecondary education, work, nonwork, military, or governmental service (such as VISTA, Action)—career guidance should help senior high school students to consider the advantages and disadvantages of each.

Career centers at the high school level should

- teach students to consider themselves in terms that include not only what they know, but also what they can do;
- work with students to use their portfolios to develop career development plans that include answers to the who, where, and how questions; long-term goals, training, and edu-

cation necessary to obtain those goals; short-term goals (what can happen in the next year); and the identification of the pertinent decision points ahead (encouraging students to see that they have decisions);

- continue to educate students, parents, schools, and the rest of the community on career development as a lifelong concept; and
- assess student readiness (in other words, where they are developmentally in terms of career development), and provide experiences, direction, knowledge, and opportunities for students who are not prepared to increase their readiness to make effective, personally meaningful career plans.

In the early 1990s, Congress found that a disproportionally large number of high school students in the United States enter the workforce without adequate academic and entry level occupational skills. Dropout rates and unemployment among youth are intolerably high. Workplaces face heightened international competition, increasing the demand for highly skilled labor. Yet the United States lacks an educational system that gives young people the knowledge, skills, abilities, and information they need to make a successful transition from school to career or to further education and training.

These and other findings precipitated the School-to-Work Opportunities Act, enacted into federal legislation in 1994. The act outlines a comprehensive education reform that offers opportunities for all the students, including those from culturally, racially, and ethnically diverse backgrounds, disadvantaged youth, and the disabled. It promotes the creation of a high-quality transition system that helps students identify and navigate career paths. It encourages the use of workplaces as active learning environments, and other school-to-work activities, such as tech-prep education, career academies, cooperative education, youth apprenticeships, school sponsored enterprises, and business education agreements.

Integrating academic and occupational learning is not the responsibility of educators alone. School-to-work is no longer a federally funded program. Many schools have adopted a Career Pathways program that is the current initiative for promoting career development. Career centers and counselors should work closely with other participants in these programs to help students develop and implement a career plan. Career centers should develop working relationships with local corporations, employers, and community agencies to ensure the effectiveness of these programs.

A career pathway is a coherent, articulated sequence of rigorous academic and career/technical courses *in an interest area of the students choosing*. Every career pathway begins in the ninth grade and leads to an associate degree, a baccalaureate degree (and beyond), an industry-recognized certificate, and/or licensure. The career pathway is developed, implemented, and maintained by a partnership involving educators (secondary and postsecondary) and employers. career pathways are available to all students (including adult learners) and lead to rewarding careers.

The essential characteristics of an ideal Career Pathway are the following:

1. **The secondary pathway component:**
   Meets state academic standards and grade-level expectations. Meets high school testing and exit requirements. Meets postsecondary (college) entry/placement requirements. Provides foundation knowledge and skills in chosen career clusters. Provides opportunities for students to earn college credit through dual/concurrent enrollment or articulation agreements.
2. **The postsecondary pathway component provides:**
   Opportunities for students to earn college credit through dual/concurrent enrollment or articulation. Alignment and articulation with baccalaureate programs. Industry-

recognized skills and knowledge in each cluster area. Opportunities for placement in the chosen career cluster at multiple exit points.

3. **Pathway partners maintain an evidence-driven culture by:**
Regularly collecting qualitative and quantitative data. Using data for planning and decision making for continuous pathway improvement. Promoting frequent, purposeful dialogue between secondary, postsecondary, and business partners.

POSTSECONDARY INSTITUTIONS

Career centers that focus on the needs of students in postsecondary institutions should provide programs or offer experiences that address a broad range of issues. It is sometimes the case that the bulk of student career development prior to postsecondary enrollment focused on getting into college or a training program and often did not consider what students might do once there (which highlights the problem of students making decisions in high school for which they are not developmentally prepared). This situation is sometimes further complicated by college career centers that primarily focus on helping students make the next transitions from the postsecondary institution to work (e.g., they primarily focus on placement rather than the much broader career development process). Often, career development in postsecondary institutions falls on the shoulders of academic advisors.

The National Academic Advising Association addressed the importance of career development and planning when discussing standards and guidelines for academic advising programs in postsecondary institutions by using the Academic Advising Standards and Guidelines created by the Council for the Advancement of Standards (CAS) for student services and development programs. (You can reach NACADA Executive Office, Kansas State University, 232

Anderson Avenue, Suite 225, Manhattan, KS 66502-2912, Phone: (785) 532-5717, Fax: (785) 532-7732, e-mail: nacada@ksu.edu, Web: http://www.ksu.edu/nacada).

These standards state that the "primary purpose of the academic advising program is to assist students in the development of meaningful educational plans that are compatible with their life goals." Further, they add that the "ultimate responsibility for making divisions about educational plans and life goals rests with the individual student. The academic advisor should assist by helping to identify and assess alternatives and the consequences of decisions." Thus it would seem appropriate for postsecondary career centers to assist students with the development of a career plan.

In terms of student needs, many postsecondary students require assistance from staff involved in career development in these four areas (adapted from Herr and Cramer 1996):

1. The selection of a major field of study
2. Self-assessment and self-analysis
3. Understanding the world of work
4. Making decisions

It is important for postsecondary career centers to recognize and reinforce the broader career development process when working with students rather than focusing on the outcome (finding a job) alone. This focus on the process of career development prepares students to meet their immediate goals as well as increasing their chances of meeting their long-term goals.

Colleges and universities have used five major approaches to meet the career development needs of students: "(1) courses, workshops, and seminars that offer structured group exercises in career planning; (2) group counseling activities that are generally less structured and emphasize broader, more affective aspects of human and career development; (3) individual counseling opportunities that accentuate diverse theoretical orientations to career concern;

(4) placement programs that culminate the career planning and decision-making process; and (5) computerized placement services." (Herr and Cramer 1996).

SUMMARY

Within an educational setting, career centers should educate students and faculty about their services and promote the expansion of career-related activities into the curricula. The centers should seek to contribute to the students' career development by

- Teaching students the skills necessary to answer the three primary questions ("Who am I?," "Where am I going?," and "How do I get there?") when they are developmentally ready to learn and use them,
- Helping faculty connect course material to the world of work, and
- Strengthening critical career development competency areas by having students apply their knowledge and skills to increasingly complex situations.

These generalized pursuits have specific manifestations at the different educational levels.

CHAPTER 7

Serving Diverse Populations

By Judith Ettinger, Ph.D.

INTRODUCTION

The American workforce is becoming more diverse. Addressing the career-related needs of diverse groups is critical to the success of all career centers. Most people would agree that a quality career center needs to foster a sense of belonging. Therefore, staff need to continually learn about topics related to diversity and to know how to use that information to create an informed and supportive environment that works for all clients (including students) and remains sensitive to the needs of each and every individual.

The literature identifies policies that tend to meet the needs of a diverse population in terms of access and acceptance. These policies include, but are not limited to

- hours of operation that offer a variety of options including evening hours, saturday hours, and early morning hours;
- distribution of career center maps and accessible routes so that all potential users know where the center is and how to get there;
- a plan to market the facility to all interested parties in a format that is accessible;

- location of the facility in the mainstream of the community/ campus or near public transportation;
- open access to resources and user-friendly files;
- materials that have been screened for stereotypes and disrespectful statements;
- access that meets the requirements of the Americans with Disabilities Act (ADA);
- materials that cover a wide range of reading levels;
- a diverse staff and/or a staff that understands and relates to individuals with diverse needs;
- a well-trained staff that knows about culturally appropriate career counseling;
- an attitude within the center that fosters broadening of employment options rather than restricting choices on the basis of image and stereotype.

This chapter will begin to discuss specific career development issues for three different groups who often use career centers: individuals with disabilities, culturally diverse groups (including limited-English proficient groups), and former offenders.

INDIVIDUALS WITH DISABILITIES

Individuals with disabilities continue to encounter a variety of difficulties when accessing career-related and employment services. They frequently run into barriers that result from a lack of respect and access. Experience tells us that it takes the collected expertise of a number of professionals to truly affect the types of change needed for equity. Career center staff can certainly contribute to this change in both their services and in the way they deliver services. It has been noted numerous times in this book that the career center environment needs to be accessible, nonthreatening, and user-friendly. What does that mean when we are talking about meeting the specific needs of individuals with disabilities? The following comments made by individuals who went to their career services office illuminate several key points that need to be taken seriously by career center staff:

> I am uncomfortable working with people because I don't know how they will react to me. I would also like to learn how to disclose my disability to potential employers. But most importantly, I want them to know about my abilities before they meet me. I don't know how to do both of those things at the same time. But I don't want to go to a job interview and have that person be surprised when I walk in with a cane.
>
> It is hard for me to even look at the word disability. I don't want to be treated differently, but the reality is that I have challenges that need to be considered. Yet I am concerned that if I reveal my disability in an interview, I won't be able to defend myself against the negative perceptions the employers would have. I feel unprepared to overcome objections and stress my skills and abilities in an interview if I choose to disclose my disability.

What career development issues are evident in these quotes?

- disclosure questions (Do I know what to say about my disability? Can I deal with insensitive questions? Will disclosing reduce my stress level or increase it? Do I want to create an atmosphere of openness and honesty from the outset, or is it better to wait until the employer knows that I can do the job successfully?)
- references to self-esteem issues
- concern about employer attitudes
- inadequacy when responding to questions in an interview
- discomfort when questions related to disability are raised
- questions about how to advocate for accommodations
- acceptance of their disability
- lack of exposure to successful role models who have similar disabilities

- lack of confidence and an inability to deal with sensitive questions.

Where can career center staff go for assistance? They can look for guidance from professionals working in the disability field and to the Americans with Disabilities Act (ADA). The ADA confronts discriminatory behaviors directed at persons with disabilities. An introduction to the strengths and relevance of the legislation follows.

The framers of the ADA established legislative support to ensure that persons with disabilities would succeed or fail on the basis of their abilities and motivation, not on the basis of having or not having a disability. Unlike previous civil rights legislation, employers are encouraged to treat individuals with disabilities differently from others only in that they are responsible for making reasonable changes in the work environment to reduce the negative impact of a disabling condition. For those working in a career center, attention should be on Title I, Employment. In this portion of the legislation, the ADA specifies that employers must provide *reasonable accommodations* to *qualified individuals* with disabilities to enable them to do the *essential functions* of a job, unless the changes impose *undue hardship* upon the employers. It is helpful to think of the ADA as a system of checks and balances in its attempt to weigh both the needs of people with disabilities and the business interests of employers. Definitions of these key terms can be read on numerous Web sites related to the ADA.

Practically speaking, this requires center staff to serve in the role of advocate for an individual with disabilities both within the actual center and also when communicating with employers. What does this look like? It is accessible parking spaces close to the center, modification of equipment that meets all requirements of the ADA, available qualified readers or sign language interpreters, higher desks and tables for wheelchair access, in addition to open aisles that allow wheelchairs into all areas of the center, and policies that allow students to remove materials from the center. It is also a policy that bars employers who discriminate from using the center for their employment needs.

When we talk about the needs of individuals with disabilities, it is important to note that most career centers use the World Wide Web as a major way to communicate. However, many Web sites are not currently accessible to those with disabilities. The problems most commonly encountered are cluttered pages, confusing navigation systems, failure to describe images, and poor color contrast between background and text. To meet the equity requirements for students with disabilities, career center staff should measure their Web sites according to the standards established in the Accessibility Guidelines 2.0 Checklist at www.w3.org/TR/2005/WD-WCAG20-20050630/checklist.html (retrieved on April 22, 2007). Examples of guidelines cited in that document include, but are not limited to:

- providing text alternatives for all non-text content
- making it easy to distinguish foreground information from the background
- making all functionality operable via a keyboard interface
- making the placement and functionality of content predictable.

Another resource that can be used to strengthen a career center's resources is the disability navigator program. This program includes a position jointly established by the Department of Labor (DOL) and the Social Security Administration (SSA) within the DOL's one-stop career centers. Navigators help people with disabilities navigate through the enormous challenges of seeking work. The position was created to better inform individuals with disabilities about the complexities of various programs that affect their abilities to gain, return to, or retain employment.

To sum up the information regarding individuals with disabilities, roles that career center staff can play when assisting individuals with disabilities include

- accepting and acting upon the notion that career centers serve all people, including those with disabilities
- establishing creative partnerships with specialized staff and rehabilitation counselors to develop an effective program by using joint expertise in meeting the specific needs of individuals with disabilities
- understanding the ADA and concepts such as *job analysis* and *reasonable accommodations,* terms used to protect the civil rights of individuals with disabilities
- being advocates with employers, students, coworkers, and employees
- knowing about resources, such as accommodations information and financial assistance, in the immediate geographic area and maintaining an information folder for easy access for the purpose of referrals
- ensuring accessibility and actively communicating about this strategy by, for example, notifying clients that materials will be prepared in alternative formats on request, by ensuring that job listings will be posted low enough to be seen by someone using a wheelchair, and by offering assistance with procuring materials and serving as scribes, interpreters, or readers
- being certain that disability-related materials are included in career libraries and career centers
- adapting policies to allow users with disabilities to take materials out of the office as needed
- monitoring attitudes of program staff toward individuals with disabilities and providing training to ensure that supportive attitudes are communicated to all individuals who participate in career development programs.

CULTURALLY DIVERSE GROUPS

What is cultural diversity? Cultural diversity speaks about one's social and cultural heritage and the concomitant differences associated with language, values, and customs. Career center staff work with individuals who come from a wide variety of cultural backgrounds. Are career center staff members able to understand the needs of various groups as they explore how they will participate in the world of work? Are they knowledgeable enough to know about barriers faced by individuals within specific cultural groups? Do they know how to right the wrongs and eliminate barriers that are associated with stereotyping and discrimination?

Career center staff need to be able to work with clients or students with as much understanding and sensitivity as possible when it comes to the values and beliefs that influence their perspectives about career planning and employment. In order to meet the needs of all individuals, it is important to recognize the need for context-sensitive career facilitation. This approach acknowledges the impact of the client's cultural context on his or her career behavior (Byars-Winston and Fouad, 2006). The literature states that it is not only important to pay attention to the client's cultural context but also to one's cultural context, because each staff person's perspectives about others are shaped by the culture he or she comes from. For example, an individual who grew up in a society that encourages women to strive as hard as men in their careers might not understand the minimal employment-related ambitions of a young woman who was raised believing that her most important work is done in her own home. An individual who was raised without participating in organized religion might not understand why a client's belief that he or she cannot work on Sunday should override an interest in the retail industry. Unless trained otherwise, individuals typically view members of their own group as positive and members outside of their group as negative. Attitudes such as this in career center staff would lead to an environment that is neither supportive nor sensitive to the needs of each individual client.

What is the solution? According to Bingham and Ward (1994), insight into one's own cultural perspective is an important first step in becoming skilled at working with culturally diverse groups. The power of one's own cultural lens is diminished, and as a result, facilitators can listen clearly to the client's needs rather than filtering those needs through their own cultural assumptions.

The Culturally Appropriate Career Counseling Model (CACCM) model was introduced by Bingham and Ward in 1994. This model includes seven steps that explicitly incorporate cultural variables into career interventions.

Step 1: Establish a culturally appropriate relationship with the client

Step 2: Identify career-related issues

Step 3: Assess the impact of cultural factors on career issues

Step 4: Set goals

Step 5: Use interventions that are culturally appropriate

Step 6: Make decisions that are culturally appropriate and address career issues

Step 7: Implement the plan and follow up.

These steps indicate the importance of examining one's personal work views and multicultural competence; they require staff members to understand their own cultural beliefs and values as well as others' (Fouad and Bingham, 1995). In sum, this means that staff need to ask themselves: What are my cultural values, and how do they influence the work that I do with my students or clients?

An Example
(Adapted Tyson and Pedersen 2000)

A high school senior who comes from a very traditional family did very well in school. During her senior advising meeting, she states that she is not going to continue her education after high school but will instead work at her father's office. She worked there during summers and liked the work and thought it was a good place for her to be. It would keep her close to home—something that was valued and respected by all members of her immediate family. No one had wandered too far from home. That was frowned upon.

A staff member at the career center asked her if she thought about getting a college-level education at a nearby university. It would allow her to continue her successes in the classroom which, in turn, could lead to a more interesting job. The client seemed puzzled by the suggestion and expressed doubt that she could afford to go to college. Information about financial aid was then shared. The student quickly left the office looking very uncomfortable.

The next morning the student's father called and told the staff person to mind her own business. The student would not be going to college but would be working in her hometown and staying close to her family until she married—end of discussion!

The questions that need to be answered are: Were the well-intentioned suggestions appropriate? Did they take into consideration the culture of the student? Did they consider her family's values and her beliefs? How can one broaden options by not stepping on the culture of another individual? How can a facilitator balance her agenda with that of the student? These are questions that need to be answered by all staff members if they are going to be effective with all populations.

In sum, staff members need to:

- become more aware of their own values and beliefs and the cultural context where they grew up
- become flexible and not defensive regarding others' values and beliefs, even though they might not agree with the staff members' own perspectives
- respect the impact of culture on the clients and students regarding career development and career decisions
- be able to match specific interventions to the unique needs of each group, while at the same time respecting cultural differences.

LIMITED-ENGLISH PROFICIENT INDIVIDUALS

As already mentioned, cultural diversity may include diversity in the primary language spoken. Capps, Fix, Passel, Ost, and Perez-Lopez (from http://www.urban.org/publications/310880.html retrieved on April 22, 2007) reported that "almost half (46 percent) of all foreign-born workers are 'limited English proficient' (LEP), according to data from Census 2000." In addition, they also found that "While time in the United States and work experience reduce the share of workers who are LEP, 29 percent of workers who have been in the country for 20 years or more can still be considered LEP." In order for LEP individuals to be fully integrated into the workforce, the National Center for Research in Vocational Education suggested in a Trends and Issues Alert (1988) that LEP individuals would

> . . . need improved job-performance skills, job-seeking skills, and cultural adjustment assistance as well as English language development. . . Among the goals of career education is equipping persons with general employability, adaptability, and promotability skills to succeed in a rapidly changing society. It also assists with career awareness, exploration, planning and decision making. Moreover, reducing bias and stereotyping is essential in order to protect freedom of career choice, an important goal in the career development of LEP persons (ERIC Document ED307380, 1988).

The U.S. Department of Justice offered the following suggestions when working with LEP individuals:

1. Create convenient and accessible points of entry for the largest language minority communities, such as a dedicated telephone number for non-English speakers.
2. Don't make assumptions regarding an individual's first language.
3. Make language identification flashcards (also known as "I Speak _____" cards) available to LEP individuals, so that they can identify their native languages for you.
4. Consider providing language assistance, even when you think an individual's English is "probably good enough."
5. When working through an interpreter, use short simple sentences that are free of idioms. Avoid compound

phrases, double negatives, rambling phrases, colloquial-isms, etc.

6. Always address the LEP individual in the first person and look at that individual (not the interpreter) during questioning.

7. Be aware that excluding an LEP person during long conversations with English-speaking individuals can sometimes convey negative messages. Wait until an interpreter or bilingual individual can be present to explain the communication to the LEP person and enable his or her participation.

8. Be creative in asking questions of the LEP individual; you may have to ask the same question several ways before eliciting a response. Don't expect your interpreter to "fill in the blanks."

9. Don't overlook and don't overestimate the power of pictures.

10. Recognize the different modes of interpretation, and the contexts in which each is appropriate.

11. Consider and plan for the possibility that an LEP person may also have a disability. (Summarized from http://www.lep.gov/lepdoc%20chapter1.htm#c and retrieved on April 22, 2007)

These Web sites might be useful for career centers when developing plans for working with LEP populations: the National Institute for Literacy (http://www.nifl.gov/), the National Assessment of Adult Literacy (http://nces.ed.gov/naal/) and Let Everyone Participate (http://www.lep.gov/).

FORMER OFFENDERS

There is a complicated relationship between crime and employment. The bottom line remains that being involved in the criminal justice system is a major obstacle to getting and keeping a good job. Research shows, however, that employment lessens the chances of recidivism. A common goal is thus to increase the employability and wages of offenders. Career center staff can be a partner in that effort.

The literature recognizes unique career-related needs for those who are in prison or who have been released from a correctional facility. Despite individual differences, this population is typically characterized by a lack of education, low self-esteem, an absence of job-seeking and job-keeping skills, a dearth of role models in the past and present, and a history of unsuccessful and unrewarding employment or no work history at all. There are programs within the career center that can certainly help an individual overcome these barriers, programs that help them not only answer questions such as who am I, where am I going, and how do I get there, but that also help these individuals explain their period of incarceration to an employer and teach them the soft skills needed to obtain and retain employment, research the labor market, put together a portfolio, and so on.

The literature also states that a critical factor in finding successful employment for a former offender is the strength of a *vocational self-concept.* This means that individuals will understand what their skills and interests are and how to match their skills and interests to employment; it means that their level of social skills and problem solving skills allow them to function efficiently on the job; it means that they have realistic expectations of the work culture. In addition, staff should focus on other barriers associated with job-keeping, which include but are not limited to, housing, childcare, transportation, and substance abuse. Staff can work to increase positive role models and access to training and education, ensure that individuals know where to find appropriate clothes for a job interview, and encourage emotional support from family and friends. Although meeting these needs will probably not fall under the auspices of career center staff, referrals to meet those needs can be an important role for staff, and they need to be trained accordingly.

It is important also to note that work-related difficulties for this specific group don't only occur within the individual. Organizational barriers also can be overwhelming, and thus represent another area in which career center staff can make an impact, eventually resulting in increased employment opportunities for former offenders. To illustrate how these needs and barriers can be translated into practice, think about what goes into preparing for a job interview. In addition to the issues common to all those preparing, former offenders must

- be able to talk comfortably about their past education and training experiences, whether they were in a correctional facility or at an institution of higher education
- be able to articulate their major duties at past jobs and use examples to illustrate skills areas, whether the skills were mastered within a correctional facility or outside
- be prepared to discuss their incarceration and, despite that setback, how they are still well suited for the job
- be prepared with copies of a résumé, transcripts, training certificates, and letters of reference that focus on strengths, not shortcomings
- have information about the place of employment where they are interviewing, along with lessons on how to complete research for future job interviews (computer access is often limited in an institution, so computer-based skills can be minimal)
- update logistical details that will start the interview on a positive note, such as getting to the interview, managing time before the interview (e.g., arriving not too early but not late), and preparing for child care

In summary, when working with former offenders, the activities and resources available should cover at least three broad areas: information about self, information about the world of education and work, and development of job-seeking and retention skills.

SUMMARY

To meet the needs of diverse populations, staff should be able to meet the following standards:

- learn to recognize and appreciate differences between self and clients
- create a multicultural environment for clients and value the backgrounds from which they come
- understand the importance of and need for positive role models who represent the client's background
- consider issues surrounding racism and stereotyping when they arise by addressing them directly
- read and research information about the historical, social, economic, and political factors affecting clients, including statistics related to workforce participation rates
- identify and promote full development of a client's potential
- recognize when differences, whether related to culture, age, or gender, are affecting communication and make appropriate adjustments.

CHAPTER 8

Adult Career Centers:
An Overview

By Jane Goodman

INTRODUCTION

Theories of adult career development have evolved in the last decades from those that assume a linear progression to those that see adult life as a response to changing personal and societal situations. Personal event and nonevent transitions join with normal life cycle changes and the aging process in a spiral of adjustment and readjustment. At the same time, they interact with economic, political, and social structures, being acted upon and acting on these structures in an ever-evolving manner. Adult development can then be seen as an interactive process of action and reaction, being affected by and affecting each individual's environment. Rarely can an individual make a career choice at a single point in time and maintain that choice until retirement. Indeed, the Bureau of Labor Statistics (2002) estimated that the average baby boomer in the United States held 9.6 different jobs from the ages of eighteen to thirty-six. Peterson (1995) has stated that "most people entering the work force today will have three to five careers and eight to ten jobs" (p. xiv). *USA Today* (July 9, 2003, p. 1B) said that in 2002, 85 percent of workers who changed jobs also switched industries, up from 11 percent in 2001, although 66 percent said they would be happy spending the rest of their career with their current employer. The basic structure of the labor force has also changed. These changes are a result of the combination of changing birthrates, the entry of large numbers of women into the workforce, the aging of the workforce, and its increased diversity (Toossi 2002). Add to this the growing numbers of Americans, including a new wave of immigration comparable to that of the beginning of the twentieth century, and you have a society in which workers are extremely unlikely to be struggling with the same career decisions and career adjustments at the same time.

People who now appear at adult career counseling centers include re-entering women; older adults who are looking for post-retirement careers; displaced workers (both white- and blue- collar) whose jobs have been eliminated through such events as plant closings, farm foreclosures, and business mergers or failures; employed men and women who are questioning the direction of their current occupation and looking for possible career alternatives; and dual-career couples whose needs are more complex than those of an individual doing career exploration.

In the sections that follow we shall provide:

- postmodern views of the needs of adults,
- a system for understanding the needs of adults in transition,
- paying attention to the needs of special populations of adults,
- elements of a good adult career counseling center,
- a description of one such center as a case study.

POSTMODERN VIEWS OF THE NEEDS OF ADULTS

Along with the growing understanding of the need for flexibility, there has been an emerging appreciation of the need for counselors, and in particular career counselors, to address meaning with their clients. This often means addressing the role of spirituality in individuals' lives, an area of inquiry that has been often overlooked. Career center staff are most likely to hear spirituality expressed through clients' subjective, personal experiences, and through their expressed need for connectedness, meaning, and transcendence. Incorporating spirituality in the counseling process is a holistic approach that addresses body, mind, and spirit, and it frequently enhances and deepens the counseling process. Looking at how clients find meaning and purpose in their lives may also tap into a hidden resource for coping with transitions. A growing body of research has documented spirituality's relationship to both physical and mental health.

Savickas (1997) deconstructed the word spirituality to remind us of its origin, which is breath or wind. The original meaning for inspire was to breathe into. It is now used to mean to hearten, to give confidence to, or to raise one's spirits. Moving beyond matching interests and skills, Savickas distinguished traditional career counseling from "career counseling that attends to the individual's spirit, . . . [that] addresses how people can use occupations and work for personal and spiritual development" (p. 6).

Postmodern thinking is typically associated with the idea of relativity in values, meaning, and truth. It presumes that each individual must discover, or uncover, truth and meaning for him or herself. Today's complex world seems to eliminate the possibility of one verity for all, regardless of how some may yearn for what they see as having been simpler times. Just as these ambiguities exist in our phenomenological world, they exist in the career development world, placing career counselors in the forefront of a demanding challenge.

The structure of the workforce is also changing in other ways to meet the needs of the twenty-first century world marketplace. Portfolio workers are a good example of the changing workplace. Possessing a set of technical and transferable skills, these individuals work for varying periods of time for one organization and then move on to another as the need for their services disappears. Organizations that employ portfolio workers have the advantage of not having workers on the payroll during times when they are not needed; they also often avoid paying all or some benefits. Workers may get paid more per hour or week, but usually have times of unemployment and often have to fund their own benefits. Retirement savings, or actually the lack thereof, are an area in which portfolio workers are particularly vulnerable.

Other workers piece together what have come to be called patch-work careers, working for a variety of organizations simultaneously, or sometimes combining an entrepreneurial activity with contractual work and consultation. We know one such worker who has a thriving flea market business combined with short- and long-term government training contracts. Counselors in private practice often combine this work with university teaching, writing, speaking, and part-time salaried work at a hospital or community mental health agency.

In actuality, this complexity and uncertainty are, for many, the good news. Although career maturity is not a linear phenomenon, people do grow and change over a lifetime. The current emphasis on preparedness has forced many young people—as young as early adolescence—to make a career decision long before they feel truly ready. Decisions made in youth or adolescence often turn out to be inappropriate as people age. Thus the need to change becomes a freedom to change. Gelatt addressed this phenomenon in his positive uncertainty theory (1991), which proposes the following: if you wait to be sure, you will never decide; if you decide too firmly, you won't be flexible enough to change as needed. His plan was based on two attitudes: 1) accepting the uncertainty of the past, present, and future, and 2) feeling positive about that uncertainty. It includes four paradoxical principles: 1) "Be focused and flexible about what you want, . . . 2) Be aware and wary about what you know . . . 3) Be objective and optimistic about what you believe . . . [and] 4) Be practical and magical about what you do" (p. 12).

A SYSTEM FOR UNDERSTANDING THE NEEDS OF ADULTS IN TRANSITION

Virtually all clients who present themselves at the doors of a career center are experiencing a transition. Defined as an event or nonevent resulting in change (Schlossberg 1981), transitions include leaving a work position, looking for a new position, or even contemplating a new position. Particularly poignant are the transitions created by the awareness that an expected event will probably not happen. For example, realizing that a longed-for promotion is unlikely (a non-event) may propel an individual to rethink career choices. Schlossberg proposed a system for analyzing such adults in transition. This system, described in Goodman, Schlossberg, and Anderson (2006), proposes that there are four critical elements in assessing an individual's transition. Easily remembered as the four S's, they are situation, self, support, and strategies. Each of these has a number of subcategories. Chapter 9 also demonstrates how these elements can be applied with adults in One-Stop Career Centers.

Situation

All individuals experience a particular situation in their own unique fashion. This experience is mediated by many situational and societal factors including the trigger, the timing and the concurrent stress being experienced, the amount of role change, and previous experience with a similar transition. Let us discuss each of these in turn.

The *trigger* for a career transition may be internal or external—that is, the individual may have chosen to leave a particular position or may be seeking a first position, or the individual may have completed a contractual assignment, may have been laid off due to a downsizing, or may have been fired for cause. Each of these situations calls for a different set of counseling interventions. For example, a person unhappy enough in a position to quit may need to explore other areas of work; a person who is downsized, may simply need job-hunting skills; a person who has left a position or is contemplating leaving a position voluntarily may also need to analyze what about the position was unsatisfying. We have found that sometimes a simple change of setting, doing the same set of tasks, solves the problem. Other times the problem is more deep-seated and relates to an individual's emotional life and has nothing to do with the actual work being performed.

The *timing and the concurrent stress* being experienced also define the uniqueness of each person's situation. When Kmart laid off a large number of people in the Detroit area, there were many situations in which both members of a couple worked for the company. These unfortunate individuals clearly had a more difficult time than those whose partner still had a job. When someone loses a job while battling a serious illness, or dealing with the serious illness of a family member, clearly stress increases accordingly. Many women return to the workplace after a divorce or after being widowed. The stress of their job search is increased by the stress of the other difficult aspects of their lives. Similarly, forced early retirement is more difficult when children are in college than when they are grown and independent. The examples are endless; the important point is that counselors working with adults give them time to discuss the fullness of their experience along with working with them to make a career decision and find a job.

The amount of *role change* created by a transition is also a relevant factor to consider in the counseling process. A stay-at-home mom entering or re-entering the workforce after a period of time will be engaging in a very different role. An entrepreneur who has lost her business and is now working for others has had a role shift that requires a major adjustment. A person who changes positions as an engineer with one hospital to being an engineer at another has little or no role change.

It is important also to explore with clients their previous *experience with a similar transition.* When that experience has had a positive outcome, most people feel more hopeful that this one will, too. When that experience has had a negative outcome, many individuals find it harder to be optimistic. It can be useful to analyze the causes of success or failure, thus providing the client with techniques to use and strategies to avoid. It is also important to explore the client's attribution for the success or failure. If the client takes blame for failures and attributes success to luck, that is a very different picture from the client who takes credit for success and attributes failure to bad luck. Using the transition model helps you investigate these aspects of a client's *situation*.

Self

The second S of the system is a client's self. In addition to looking at such parameters as mental health or ego strength, you may want to explore the *salience* of work in clients' lives, the *balance* among work, home life, and leisure, and their *resilience*.

For some clients, paid work is central to their identity, to their sense of self. For others, it is a way to make a living, while they find meaning in their lives through avocations, family, or spiritual pursuits. The *salience* of work, therefore, helps determine the importance of a work transition and the emotions that will be attached to it. Similarly, the *balance* of work in an individual's life is relevant to understanding the power of the transition being faced. *Balance* is often the behavioral enactment of *salience*, although it is certainly possible for someone to work few hours at a job for which he or she cares a lot and many at one that has little salience.

We described the importance, earlier, of previous experience with transitions, in particular similar transitions. A client's ability to bounce back from struggle, what we call here resilience, is increasingly being hailed in the literature as a central aspect of positive coping (cf. Bosworth and Walz, 2005).

Support

The third S in our quartet is support. Elements of support include that which is internal, that is *feeling positive about oneself*, or having a sense of self-esteem and self-efficacy. It may not be true that people can do something simply because they think they can; it is certainly true that people who think they can't do something can't. Positive self-beliefs may come from many sources, but one is certainly the *encouragement* of others. If clients do not know where they can find encouragement, it can be helpful to identify some, and at the least, the counselor should be one. Some other aspects of support may be more tangible, such as *referrals,* networking help, *information,* and *practical help,* such as preparing a résumé or driving a client to a job interview.

Helping clients articulate their support system may also help them look at their stress system. Plans to enhance the one and diminish the other can be an important counseling strategy. Teaching support access skills and stress reduction skills are important components of the didactic aspects of career services.

Strategies

Finally, as we look at the fourth S, we begin to examine strategies clients can use to manage their career transition. When clients can *modify the situation*—by finding new work, for example, or entering into training for another line of work—they gain control not only over the actual situation, but often over the emotions surrounding it. When they cannot change it, or cannot change it right away or in their preferred manner, they may need to find ways to *change the meaning* of the problem. Counselors can help their clients reframe a transition as an opportunity for growth, a chance to take some desired risks, or a chance to show their mettle. It is important, however, that reframing not be used to minimize the discomfort or grief associated with the transition. And finally, counselors and other career center personnel can teach clients responses that help to *manage stress* after it has occurred.

PAYING ATTENTION TO THE NEEDS OF SPECIAL POPULATIONS OF ADULTS

It is clearly beyond the scope of this chapter to address any or all special populations of adults in any detail. For a thorough handling of this topic, please see, Herr, Cramer, and Niles (2004). We will also not address the issue of adults with disabilities, as that important topic requires much fuller explication than we can give it here and is discussed in Chapter 7.

Older Adults

Older adults who require career counseling may be planning for retirement from a primary job, but they often also need to earn a living or hope to find work to contribute to society or meet affiliation needs. Whether the older adult is seeking paid or unpaid work, wants full- or part-time employment, or has another motivation for seeking the services of a career center, career counselors need to follow their standard practice of exploration, reality testing, and decision making. The needs of older people are as varied as the needs of the young, if not more so. Financial considerations may be different, but they are still important. It may be humorous to a twenty-something counselor to think of a sixty-something client making long-term plans, but with increased longevity has come increased desire among some to work as long as they are physically and mentally able to do so. Schlossberg, in *Retire Smart, Retire Happy* (2004), has described six types of retirement, and that number does not include those who continue to work at the same pace in the same occupation, as many do. Clearly, older adults have complex needs as the their life unfolds.

Displaced Workers

The changed structure of the workforce has resulted in a large number of displaced workers now facing decisions about new careers and confronting a job search, often for the first time in their lives. The headlines daily announce thousands of workers laid off as companies downsize or attempt to stave off bankruptcy. Spinoff reductions occur in related industries, also leading to unemployment for many. For example, when General Motors and Ford announce large lay-offs, auto parts suppliers follow suit. Many of these people moved into their previous work lives without much conscious thought and find themselves ill-equipped to decide upon and find new positions. Counselors need to target their strategies to the different psychological stages experienced by most displaced workers. The stages of grief after a lost job can mirror grief over the death of a loved one. Studies confirm the negative effects of involuntary job loss on the well-being of individuals and families; unemployment has been correlated with increases in substance abuse, mental health problems, physical illnesses, and spousal abuse (Herr, Cramer, and Niles 2004).

Amundson (1996) proposed 12 reframing strategies for clients struggling with unemployment. These approaches, divided into looking at the past, present, and future include: normalization, a look at accomplishments, transferable skills and attitudes, positive affirmation, attempts to externalize the problem, and limits on negative thinking. They are all designed to help clients "attain new perspectives on themselves and the labor market" (p. 161). These kinds of emotional issues are the reason this author believes that career centers need to have trained professional counselors on their staffs, and that the non-counselors should have special training in recognition of emotional issues and in referral resources and techniques.

Dual-Career Couples

In more and more two-parent families, both members of the couple are engaged in paid employment. As pointed out by Niles, Herr, and Hartung (2002) and by Hansen (2002), family structures are changing. The increase in single-parent families means that there is no option except work for the head of the household. In other, more affluent situations, many men and women choose jobs with less commitment during the time their children are small. Part of the dual-career negotiation process may be whether both members of the couple or either will make what may be seen as a sacrifice during these years. Both members of the couple will need to look at reduced income if one works fewer hours or not at all. Many people, later in their lives and careers, find themselves needing to take care of aging or ill parents or other relatives.

Increasingly, career counselors are being sought by dual-career couples who have complex career planning issues because of their interdependence. In the past, career planning has been viewed as an individual activity, but for both men and women in dual-career relationships, career decisions cannot be made without taking into consideration the connection between work and family roles. Consequently, both partners must be involved in the career counseling process to deal with the issues of balancing roles and demands, juggling responsibilities, and the careful planning of career transitions. Today's global marketplace often adds a particularly poignant dilemma for many. One member of a couple may be asked or expected to work in another country for a significant period of time. What does the other member do? Work rules in the new country might prohibit him or her from working. Again, counselors in an adult career center may hear these concerns and need to help their client figure out an appropriate strategy.

ELEMENTS OF A GOOD ADULT CAREER COUNSELING CENTER

America's Career Resource Network (ACRN) http://www.acrnetwork.org/ncdg.htm (retrieved April 22, 2007) has updated the guidelines originally developed by the National Occupational Information Coordinating Committee (NOICC). These guidelines can provide a blueprint for career centers to follow in developing their planned program of activities and are listed in Chapter 1.

Each of these competencies implies a number of activities and counseling interventions. For example, to "use accurate, current, and unbiased career information during career planning and management," a person must 1) identify employment trends that affect career plans, 2) be prepared to respond to changing employment trends, and 3) evaluate career management plans relative to changes in employment trends (ACRN, retrieved April 22, 2007).

Niles and Harris-Bowlsbey suggested that clients coming to a career center should end their experience able to, "1) Describe realistically the transition they have chosen to make. 2) Identify forces for and forces against accomplishing the change. 3) State a definite career goal and how they plan to reach it" (p. 277). Although many clients may not have chosen to make the transition that brings them into a center, the goals they outline may serve as a helpful way to evaluate a center's program.

Over the years the concept of what constitutes career development for adults has changed and expanded. Many of these changes have come in response to an increasingly rapidly changing society where "future shock" is indeed a present reality. Many people are employed at poverty-level wages, and all face a changing definition of job security. These changing notions of the meaning of work and expectations of the work environment have been amply discussed in the media and in top selling works such as Rifkin's *The End of Work* (1995) and Bridges's *JobShift* (1994).

According to Richard Bolles's *What Color is Your Parachute,* about 10 percent of U.S. workers change careers yearly. Of these, 5.3 million changed voluntarily, 1.3 million changed involuntarily, and 3.4 million changed careers for a mixture of voluntary or involuntary reasons. These changes mean that "career development services are now concerned to help individuals not to *choose* careers but to *construct* them" (Watts 2000, p.13).

While not the focus of this chapter, it is important to keep in mind the influence of both family and culture on career development. Evans and Rotter (2000) identified areas to consider when working with families from a variety of cultures: socioeconomic status, language barriers, generational conflicts, and discrimination (pp. 68-69). Clearly, all of these have an influence on career decision making. They conclude, "Choosing a job is but the end result of a dynamic process of self-awareness, exploration, planning, and decision making. This process can only be effective when cultural, ethnic, and familial themes are addressed" (p.70).

Furthermore, it is in the best interest of a global society that career development services are available to adults. Watts (2000) argued that career development services should meet the needs of both individuals and the wider society—that is, "that they represent a public good as well as a private good" (p. 11). He stated that these benefits can be organized into two categories, economic efficiency and social equity. It is arguable that the *economic efficiency* of a society can be improved if its citizens make better career decisions. There will be less waste in education and training programs if they are well chosen; individuals are more likely to complete the programs successfully if there is a good match with their skill and interest level. Furthermore, good occupational information can assist individuals in choosing work where they are more likely to find employment, again increasing the efficiency of the system.

Social equity is advanced when individuals make occupational decisions based on job availability, training availability, and their own personal attributes, rather than on social class, differing abilities, or other potentially disadvantaging characteristics. Lack of access to good information has been endemic in several societal substrata; lack of assistance in decision making has also pervaded the lives of many people. Having effective and available career assistance could mitigate both of these circumstances. (For a further discussion of social class and other equity concerns, see Bluestein 2006.)

Globalization is affecting not only the ways organizations conduct business, but also the need for individuals to have access to career information to help meet their needs. Reardon, Lenz, Sampson, and Peterson (2000) believe that the ever-increasing number of multinational companies will greatly affect work activity and production around the world. For example, companies, work, and production will move effortlessly across international borders. The concept of a strictly American company or product will be nonexistent. Career information and knowledge about growth in both occupations and industries will be necessary for individual career planning for future employment.

Organizations are becoming increasingly concerned about employees having access to career development services. According to Gilley and Eggland (1997), many performance problems on the job are career related. They state that employees often feel trapped, stagnated, or overlooked in their present jobs or occupations. Many people feel little pleasure in their work, and they concur that this contributes to increased stress and lowered output. They conclude that many people do not work to their full potential and often fail to meet organizational expectations.

It would be helpful if organizations were able to provide career services on-site, but most do not. It then becomes the responsibility of the individual to find career services in the community. Acquisition of career information not only helps individuals to further their careers, but also meets the needs of the organization. Gilley and Eggland (1997) emphasize this by stating that it is the employee who is responsible for his or her career planning. Career centers, therefore, fill an important role.

A National Public Radio report (August 23, 2000) stated that only a third of workers in California work at typical nine-to-five jobs, salaried by the organization for whom they work. The rest are freelance, portfolio, temporary, leased, on-call, interim, or contract workers. According to an Upjohn Institute Study, flexible staffing arrangements were used at 78 percent of organizations. Some 46 percent of companies used workers from temp agencies, and 44 percent used independent contractors (Reardon, Lenz, Sampson, Peterson 2000).

These new work modalities meet the needs of many workers for autonomy and flexibility, and they clearly meet the needs of employers for a flexible, just-in-time, workforce. Such new work structures, with their lack of a predictable income, benefits, or retirement plans, create insecurity and distress for many workers. While higher paid workers may be able to weather this situation and purchase their own benefits, lower paid workers often live in hopes of staying healthy and without provision for retirement. A Bureau of Labor Statistics study reported in the *Monthly Labor Review,* that more than 60 percent of contingent workers preferred to have permanent jobs (Reardon, Lenz, Sampson, Peterson 2000).

DESCRIPTION OF ONE SUCH CENTER

The Adult Career Counseling Center (ACCC) was founded in 1982 as a community service of Oakland University, to "provide career exploration and planning opportunities to community adults at no cost" (Miller, Hall, Kelemen, and Klinck 2006, p. 6). Students in the master's level counseling program are employed for two years as graduate assistant advisers to implement the program. They are supervised by a faculty member in the counseling department, but take full responsibility for the day-to-day operations of the center. More than 12,000 clients have used the services of the ACCC since its inception. The center is supported by Oakland University funds, with the counseling department contributing the services of the faculty supervisor through released time from teaching.

Originally planned as a computer-dependent service, with only minimal assistance available from center staff, the ACCC has evolved into a true career counseling center, with the typical client coming for three to five sessions and taking advantage of a variety of services. These include talking with the adviser, using computer-assisted and Internet-based career guidance programs, taking paper-and-pencil inventories, conducting traditional and Internet-based job search activities, and using role rehearsal and videotape to practice job interviews. All sessions are provided individually or in small groups and face-to-face. Although job placement is not provided, clients often seek help in resume preparation and in learning to use the Internet to identify openings. Referrals are made to one-stop centers, to vocational rehabilitation services, and to Oakland University's Counseling Practicum Center.

The mission of the ACCC is to

- provide career exploration and planning opportunities to community adults at no charge
- train faculty, staff, and students in the use of computer-assisted career guidance programs
- support research efforts for a better understanding of the career development needs of adults.

Its goals are "to provide career exploration and planning opportunities to community adults at no charge, to train faculty, staff, and students in the use of computer-assisted career guidance programs, and to support research efforts for a better understanding of the career development sphere, ultimately promoting better career guidance practices for adults" (Miller et al, p. 7).

The center is marketed through traditional means, such as press releases to radio and television (especially cable television), as well as through an annual open house held during National Career Development Month. The majority of clients, however, hear about the center's services through word-of-mouth, usually from past clients who were pleased with the service they received. The center is open 60 hours per week, including four evenings and Saturday. These extended hours provide access for working adults and those who need to wait for a partner to return from work to take care of young children.

Additionally, the center is expected to provide training to counseling practicum students and part-time faculty in the use of computer- and Internet-assisted career guidance programs, as well as to conduct research that supports the center's mission of providing career guidance assistance to adults. The center's annual reports for the last several years are available on line at the ACCC Web site: http://www2.oakland.edu/oakland/ouportal/index.asp?item=5125&site=110. Its work is described more fully in Goodman and Savage (1999).

SUMMARY

This overview provided introductory material on adult career development. We discussed a postmodern view of the needs of adults and described a perspective for understanding the needs of adults in transition. These nonlinear approaches were provided to underline the interactive process of adjustment and readjustment. Also critical is understanding the needs of special populations of adults (which will also be discussed in future chapters). Elements of a good adult career counseling center include attention to personal/social development, educational attainment and lifelong learning, and career management.

CHAPTER 9

One-Stop Career Centers for Adults

By Judith Ettinger, Ph.D.

areer centers are designed to provide a full range of programs for those looking for career assistance. This includes individuals who want to know more about their skills and their interests, those who are looking for a job, those who are laid off, and those who need to retrain to be employable in a new occupation. This chapter will discuss tips that can help center staff design and deliver the kinds of programs that will meet these needs.

In this chapter, we are talking about services and programs that meet the needs of adults who typically come to a career center. Generally these individuals are over the age of 18, and they tend to exhibit one or more of the following characteristics:

- possess a lack of awareness of the wide range of occupations in the workplace
- lack direction, goals, and/or a plan of action
- have not kept pace with changing job technologies, procedures, and practices
- have a single career orientation and have not thought about other options
- lack an understanding of the benefits and problems that accompany a career change

- feel unfulfilled in their present circumstances and are searching for challenge and meaning in their work

Additional barriers faced by adults might include transportation, housing, family issues (including day care), language and literacy deficits, limited education, financial difficulties, low self-esteem, age discrimination, health problems, a prison record, and disabilities. In an attempt to help career center staff that serve adults, this chapter will discuss the National Career Development Guidelines, a theory by Nancy Schlossberg that focuses on transitions, and a plan for working with adults as they look for satisfaction in the workplace.

HOW CAN THE NATIONAL CAREER DEVELOPMENT GUIDELINES (NCDG) ASSIST?

How does one organize a career center to meet the diverse needs of adults? The National Career Development Guidelines are designed for that purpose. They represent a major effort by the U.S. Department of Education to foster excellence in career development for people of all ages, genders, and cultural backgrounds. The NCDG offer direction by providing a blueprint of career development goals that need to be mastered in order to make a "good" career decision. The goals are grouped into three broad domains: personal/social development, educational achievement, and career management. There are a total of 11 goals and a list of indicators under each goal. These goals and indicators dictate what happens in the career center. All indicators are written at three levels of learning. The first level is the knowledge stage (K) where one begins, the second is the application stage (A), and the third is the reflection stage (R). These goals and indicators can be used as a road map to create and deliver services to all adults. For a complete list of the indicators under each goal, see www.acrnetwork.org/ncdg.htm.

National Career Development Guidelines (List of Goals)
Personal Social Development Domain
- Develop an understanding of yourself to build and maintain a positive self-concept.

- Develop positive interpersonal skills, including a respect for diversity.
- Integrate personal growth and change into your career development.
- Balance personal, leisure, community, learner, family, and work roles.

Educational Achievement and Lifelong Learning Domain
- Attain educational achievement and performance levels needed to reach your personal and career goals.
- Participate in ongoing, lifelong-learning experiences to enhance your ability to function effectively in a diverse and changing economy.

Career Management Domain
- Create and manage a career plan that meets your goals.
- Use a process of decision-making as one component of career development.
- Use accurate, current, and unbiased career information during career planning and management.
- Master academic, occupational, and general employability skills in order to obtain, create, maintain, and/or advance your employment.
- Integrate changing employment trends, societal needs, and economic conditions into your career plans.

An example of how one would apply the National Career Development Guidelines follows. One member of the career center staff goes into a local alternative high school twice a month and works with students who are at risk of not graduating. She works with them on their employment needs. When they graduate, many typically express an interest in getting a full-time job. Others plan on going to the local community college part time while they work. The students don't really know how to go about looking for a job. The staff person needs to design a program to meet their needs. How does she do that? The NCDG can help. Upon looking at the NCDG, she concludes that it is important to work on the fourth goal in the Career Management Domain (master academic, occupational, and general employability skills in order to obtain, create, maintain, and/or advance your employment). At the awareness stage, she begins by working on the following indicators:

- identify job-seeking skills
- know that each student has skills that can be transferred from one occupation to another
- identify the advantages and challenges of employment in a nontraditional occupation

Once these are mastered, the class moves to the application stage and focuses on specific indicators by having each student:

- demonstrate skills by writing a résumé and cover letter, completing a job application, interviewing for a job, and pursuing employment leads
- give specific examples of his or her transferable skills

The NCDG do not provide the lessons to teach, but as seen in this example, they can serve as a road map by delineating the goals and indicators that a student or client must master in order to be ready. They provide the outline needed to organize and plan services. In addition, the NCDG can help to determine whether programs adequately provide the appropriate services, covering all goals and indicators, to meet those specific needs.

IS THERE A THEORY THAT CAN HELP DESIGN AND DELIVER SERVICES TO ADULTS IN TRANSITION?

Adults who use career centers are, in one way or another, in the middle of a transition. If staff understand the components of those transitions, they can provide an approach to meet the needs of the individual experiencing some type of change. Transition theories, by definition, focus on specific points in time. A theory by Nancy Schlossberg (1989) can lead staff to an understanding of how one is coping with a transition and the strategies that need to be used for a successful transition (as was mentioned in Chapter 8). Schlossberg's theory is based on four major assumptions:

- Life is characterized by change.
- Transitions are events or nonevents that cause changes. An *event* is something that happens, such as graduating from college, getting a job, or getting married. A *nonevent* is something that a person expects and wants to happen but never does, such as not getting a coveted job, not becoming a parent, or not getting a promotion. Both events and nonevents can result in a change in roles, relationships, and routines.
- Transitions vary in the effects that they have on people.
- Success in life is highly related to a person's ability to cope with transitions.

Schlossberg's theory becomes active as she talks about the four S's. It is these four S's that not only help to define the transitions, but consequently point to possible solutions to overcome problems that result from them. The four S's are:

- situation
- self
- supports
- strategies developed from the previous S's and based on an understanding of the prior discussions

She defines *situation* as the current status of the transition in terms of its severity, its timing, the amount of control one has, how long it will last, and what else is going on to complicate or ease one's ability to cope with the transition. The situation can be understood by answering the following questions:

- How severe is the situation? How much change is required in roles, relationships, and routines?
- What is the timing of the transition? Is it happening at a good time or a bad time?
- How much control does the person have over the transition? Are there some options from which to choose?
- How permanent is the transition? How long will these new situations last?
- What else is going on in the person's life? Is energy being spent on transitions in other life roles at the same time?

When talking about *self,* Schlossberg focuses on the strengths, experiences, and resources of the individual, such as coping behaviors, decision-making skills, the need (or lack of need) for immediate gratification, the ability to take responsibility, a strong self-concept, and/or the knowledge about how one can fit into the work world. The following questions can help define self:

- What is the individual's general outlook on life? Does he or she tend to see the cup as half full or half empty?
- Where is the individual's center of control? Does he or she believe that life can be largely controlled from within, or that people are pawns of fate, controlled by external powers or events?
- Does the person possess such skills as being able to manage stress, be assertive, and make decisions?
- Does the person have a track record of being able to face transitions and deal with them effectively? How much resilience or adaptability does he or she have?

Schlossberg's theory talks about *support* in terms of the assistance that is available from family, friends, employers, and financial resources.

Questions to ask regarding the availability of support could include:

- Does the individual have friends and family who can help him or her get through the transition?
- Is there sufficient money or other material resources to carry the individual through the transition period?
- Are there agencies or other service providers that can provide support through the transition?

As she moves to the fourth S, *strategies,* Schlossberg looks at ways to cope with the transition, given what was discovered during an examination of self, situation, and support. She usually includes an action plan as one possible strategy. In the *strategy* step, the following questions might be relevant:

- What are some ways to see this situation in a different and more positive light?
- Are there some inner resources that could be further developed?
- Are there some additional support people or agencies that can help?
- What are some alternatives to move the person out of this situation?
- Which of these alternatives seems to be the best?
- What are the steps that need to be followed to pursue the selected alternative?
- What is the time frame for accomplishing each of these steps?

Once the information is collected on an individual's needs, it is time to move to the next steps: setting goals and designing an action plan that moves one toward those goals. According to Schlossberg, an *action plan* maps out what must be accomplished in order to achieve a goal. The plan typically includes both long-term and short-term goals, as well as alternative routes and back-up plans. Once the action plan is written, it is time to begin plowing through the small steps that will move an individual toward his or her goals.

HOW CAN SERVICES BE PROVIDED TO ALL WHO ARE IN NEED?

One of the difficulties of working in a center that is open to the public is the large number of individuals who walk through the door needing services. Everyone needs to be attended to and respected as a client. Sampson (2007) developed a service delivery model that differentiates between the types of services individuals need. This service delivery design is summarized below. The goal of the Sampson model is to provide the right resources, used by the right people, with the right level of support, at the lowest possible cost.

Readiness for Career Decision Making

Given the limited financial resources available and the large number of individuals needing assistance, one needs to first assess an individual's readiness for career decision making as either high, medium, or low. The three levels of service in the Sampson model are self-help, brief staff-assisted, and individual case-managed. The level of service provided to individuals varies depending on their level of readiness to make decisions. Note that individuals can move from one level of service delivery to another based on their use of resources and services.

Self-Help Services

Self-help services involve self-guided use of self-assessment, information, and instructional materials and media in a career resource room or on a Web site. Signage in the resource room, resource guides, Web sites, and the availability of support from a practitioner or administrative staff member when needed are essential elements of good self-help services. Support is provided through an orientation, and a follow-up assessment determines if resources were available to meet needs. Practitioners and support staff typically monitor the progress of individuals in a career resource room to help identify those individuals who actually require more substantial assistance.

Brief Staff-Assisted Services

Brief staff-assisted services involve practitioner-guided use of assessment, information, and instructional materials and media in a career resource room, classroom, or group setting for adolescents and adults with *moderate* readiness for career decision making. An action plan is often used to identify and prioritize goals and related resources and services that will be used to make an informed occupational, educational, training, or employment choice.

Individual Case-Managed Services

Individual case-managed services involve practitioner-guided use of assessment, information, and instructional materials and media in an individual office, classroom, or group setting for adolescents and adults with *low* readiness for career decision making. Counseling is usually a key element of individual case-managed services.

WHAT RESOURCES ARE TYPICALLY AVAILABLE IN A ONE-STOP CAREER CENTER?

This section focuses solely on the resources developed by the Department of Labor for their one-stop career centers. The U.S. Department of Labor launched the one-stop career center initiative in 1994 in response to the perception that federal training and other employment-related service programs were fragmented, duplicative, and difficult to access by consumers and employers. The one-stop centers were designed to create a continuum of services, including both federal and state training programs. The Employment and Training Administration has worked over the past decade to develop an electronic program of resources referred to as America's Workforce Network, which may be found at http://www.doleta.gov. Other Web sites that are part of that system include the following:

- America's Job Bank (http://www.ajb.org) is a pool of active job opportunities listed by major corporations and small businesses throughout the United States. Job seekers can post their résumés on this site.

- America's Learning Xchange (http://www.alx.org) provides information on career exploration, training, education, testing, assessment, and other career tools, such as certification information for specific occupations.
- America's Career InfoNet (http://www.acinet.org) includes information on job trends, wages, and national and local labor markets, as well as occupational, economic, and demographic data.
- O*NET Online (http://online.onetcenter.org/) is a database that describes a wide variety of occupations, their required skills, and their earnings potential. There are also several career exploration assessments that are part of the system, including the Interest Profiler, the Work Importance Locator, and the Ability Profiler.

SUMMARY

Adults face unique career issues and concerns, and one-stop career centers were developed to meet their needs. Career centers that work with adults need to focus on self-knowledge, providing information that describes and defines the workplace and work environment, and offering a system for integrating this information so the individual is prepared to seek and keep a job. Resources described in this chapter to help staff include the National Career Development Guidelines, transition theory, and a model of differentiated services.

CHAPTER 10

Corporate Career Centers

By Ken Patch

INTRODUCTION

Corporate career centers have a unique and distinctively different orientation from career centers found on the college campus or embedded in the one-stop centers or of other employment centers or agencies. Career centers in educational institutions, especially secondary and postsecondary, serve an "itinerant" population, one that comes into the system for a varied amount of time. Members of this itinerant population form temporary relationships with the service provider and, as in the case of students, for a prescribed length of time. Following graduation from the institution, a former student can renew the relationship, but that renewal is based on the length of time that it takes to fulfill the identified needs. Their needs might be for self-assessment, decision making about the direction to take to achieve identified goals, or, specifically, to find employment, to get back into school, or to make other career and occupational decisions that would again lead the individual away from the service provider with no further attachments.

Similarly, adult programs and processes also typically serve this itinerant population through one-stop career centers. The population enters the career center for general or specific needs fulfillment and once these needs are met, the participants separate from the institution, career center, or one-stop service centers to go on their way. With the separation typically goes a severance of relationship and even allegiance as the work is finished until the need again arises, if ever.

Corporate career centers serve employees and, because of that distinction, are unique in their focus, mission, and delivery of service. The focus of this chapter is on the corporate career centers that have moved beyond the other types of career services for adults.

HISTORY OF CORPORATE CAREER CENTERS

Corporate career centers came about through an evolutionary process that began sometime after *Sputnik* shook up the American political and educational systems. The race to be number one in space challenged American educational systems and American industrial organizations to rethink the way that work and preparation for work were being done.

Following World War II, large numbers of men and women were released from the military and from the industries that supported the war effort. Until the United States could retool as a consumer economy, there was a surplus labor pool and a lack of jobs to employ all of the veterans and displaced war-effort employees.

Of course, this period followed the Great Depression era, which had already led to the development of employment offices and testing programs such as the General Aptitude Test Battery (GATB). These employment services served as the foundation for what was to come after the end of World War II relative to career centers.

One of the efforts to deal with the large number of veterans was the passage of the GI Bill of Rights. "The newly created 'GI Bill' financially allowed eligible veterans to go to school to learn technical skills and to attain diplomas and degrees at all levels" (Patch 2000, p. 9).

With a mass enrollment of veterans in postsecondary schools, development or expansion of career centers became a necessity. These career centers, located in many cases on the campuses of colleges, were patterned after the state employment services model, to incorporate testing and counseling for career decision making. However, these new school-based programs initially focused on decisions about college education or training majors. Decision making about job placement that used the related career services—such as how to find a job, how to prepare applications, and so on—were not even needed until the first wave of students approached graduation. At that point, the career centers took on a new look, which in some cases seems to have continued to today, where the number of job placements became the measurement criterion for evaluation.

The corporate world in the United States benefited from the expanding supply of well-trained and educated production workers and technical experts. Men and women of that era had strong work ethics and were very productive workers. However, technology and its applications began to escalate in the 1960s and 1970s. Production lines began to replace people with simple robots to do simple jobs. Changes in technology began to affect employment patterns. Companies were later described as having a psychological contract with employees, and were thought to have a responsibility to provide jobs from entry until retirement, as that had previously been the experience. However, the elimination of jobs due to technological innovations displaced people, creating a challenge to the psychological contract.

Even though employment changes were beginning to take place, the concept of career development in organizations continued to model earlier developmental models. According to Zunker (2002), "In the 1970s and 1980s, career development in organizations was related to upward mobility with predictable promotions and job descriptions. An employee aspired to reach the top of the pyramid in an orderly progression of steps" (p. 575). Career paths were identifiable, and succession planning happened across management levels, however probably not in the formal way it is now orchestrated by management and human resources organizations.

In the 1980s, with the employment changes beginning to take place, career paths began to be less identifiable and more uncertain. And companies, in cost-cutting and management-control efforts, began to remove layers of management. Changes from the old models of organizational structure, which resembled pyramids, to much flatter models created other changes in the organizations. Workers went from having well-defined but narrow job descriptions to broader roles that required more demanding skills (Zunker, 2002).

Conscientious employers struggled with the need to serve faithful and productive employees. This need served as the basis for the development of corporate career centers. "In the search for process assistance in this area, business and industry turned to employment services and to colleges to identify best practices" (Patch 2000, p. 10). This search gave birth to the early corporate career centers within the companies themselves. These centers looked very much like the career centers found on college campuses, and they typically provided very similar services, including job placement across organizations.

Massive layoffs of the 1980s reinforced the need for employee career services, but also led to or contributed to the rapid growth in private career development services and the shifting of responsibility for career development services to consulting companies outside of the business (Patch 2000, p. 10). A number of companies became specialists in providing external transition services for displaced workers, providing assistance with résumé writing, interviewing skills, job search strategies, and ways to deal with the emotional impact of job loss. Some companies contracted with these outside businesses to provide this range of services both on-site and in remote locations where coworkers would not see the individuals coming and going for career assistance.

An alternative to the use of external organizations was the development of internal career-transitions centers. Knowdell, Branstead, and Moravec (1996) reported on strategic transition options that affected both individuals and the organizations involved. The purpose of such centers, according to these authors, could be to help displaced employees move into new jobs that pay well and use their skills and abilities, regain their positive self-esteem, and reduce the loss of financial and emotional security (p. 167).

CORPORATE CAREER CENTERS: UNIQUE AND PURPOSEFUL

In the early days of corporate career centers, outside consultants were often called in to provide the career counseling, to offer résumé writing or other services, or to design the internal service programs. However, in some cases senior managers would assign someone internally, often without qualifications or background, to "fix the career problem." Their backgrounds ranged from engineers, physical education teachers, English majors, to newly arrived, inexperienced human resources personnel. This often occurred following the analysis of results on employee satisfaction surveys, tools commonly used in corporations to take the attitudinal temperature of employees. Fortunately, as businesses became more sophisticated in career work, they came to realize that both employee needs and business needs had to be addressed, and that the individuals best prepared to lead the career center effort were probably those who had educational backgrounds and/or extensive experience in career work.

In recognition of the needs of users of corporate career centers, three models have typically evolved for the operation of these centers. Already addressed is the model of having the center provided through contract with an outside company and having the center external to the campus of the corporation.

A second model is one of partnership with the career center of a college or university. Within that model, the employees are referred to the college career center for assistance with career development assessment, résumé writing, interviewing skills, and so on. In turn, the corporation typically provides support through career fairs, employment opportunities, funding of meeting room facilities at the college campus, internship opportunities, and other resources uniquely available from the corporation. Chapter 11 discusses career center partnerships in greater detail.

The third model of corporate career centers is the internal center run by the company itself. This was the model of Motorola and many other companies, such as two that will be presented in the following paragraphs. The *Career Planning and Adult Development (CPAD) Journal* identified nine corporate career centers as being representative of the best programs in the country in a special issue on "Innovations in Corporate Career Centers" (2000). This recognition was based on the types of programs and services and the approaches to delivery, through on-ground and Internet based modalities. Of these programs, three are discussed here.

Corporate career centers are different from other types of career centers. Career centers developed in companies serve the employees of that company. This may sound simplistic, but it is very important. Businesses tend to do things that contribute to their profitability. Thus, the career centers in many corporations are seen as investments rather than as cost centers. From an investment standpoint, the company expects that whatever is provided at the career center will yield a financial return. Financial return can be anticipated through such measurables as employee morale, satisfaction, attendance, productivity, and retention.

Career centers in companies are also dedicated to meeting the needs of the company. The most effective career centers are those that serve the needs of the employees and the needs of the company in an almost seamless manner.

One such program can be found at Eli Lilly and Company. Tom Heady (2000) was charged with the task of developing its career center in the early 1990s. Heady led the benchmarking effort that was common then, as many companies raced to come on board with their own career centers to provide employee career services. According to Heady, they "developed a Career Planning Workshop to focus on transferable skills and . . . life elements for career decision-making" (Heady 2000, p. 51). He went on to identify other programs and services, including a resource library, a program to pay for external education, a program to develop skills-training opportunities, to incorporate career assessment, and to develop a workshop to gain the support of management at the top levels.

About the same time that the Eli Lilly Career Center was developed, Marsha Boettger was leading the creation of a career development resources center at DaimlerChrysler. Like other companies, "In response to an employee opinion survey, administered in late 1992, a decision was made by Corporate Human Resources senior management to launch a company sponsored career center" (Boettger 2000, p. 46).

Employee input and suggestions were taken into account as programs and resources were developed to provide a variety of job related resource materials, assistance with college planning, development of in-house personal history records, language books and tapes, and information on cultural differences, legal and regulatory requirements, and business practices in different countries. The overall purpose of the career development resources center was that it "aligns with the overall corporate strategy, supports future competitive success, increases workforce development and maximizes the potential of all employees" (Boettger 2000, p. 49).

The third representative career center program was developed by Gary Recchion of Recchion & Associates. In partnership with the Honeywell human resources department senior staff, Recchion began the planning phase of the employee career center progam in 1995 (Recchion 2000). The career development objectives were directly aligned with key business drivers and strategies "to build a world-class workforce by creating an environment that promotes employee delight and enables the development of skills and competencies that drive business goals and priorities" (Recchion 2000, p. 75).

The Recchion & Associates partnership with Honeywell human resources represents a partnership between a corporation and an external contractor in which the career center is located internally but operated by an external company. The partnership, however, is seamless. To an observer either within the corporation or from the outside, the employee career center would appear to be run by the company. This is a tribute to both parties as a demonstration of the effectiveness of the alignment of organizational needs with employee development and retention.

These three programs demonstrate the uniqueness and purposefulness of corporate career centers. They are dedicated to meeting the needs, goals, and objectives of the company while recognizing that a well-trained, developed, and skillful workforce is necessary for corporate success. And these programs also recognize that a stable workforce is vital, thus demonstrating the need to retain employees consistent with organizational needs. In contrast, recipients of career services in traditional career centers can be viewed as being "itinerant" or "transient," the goal of corporate career centers is to develop a workforce that will continue to contribute to the company's productivity and provide a high return on investment as a result of career center participation.

DEVELOPING CORPORATE CAREER CENTERS

In this section, we will focus on developmental steps relative to building corporate career centers offered by Richard Knowdell (1996).

Step 1: Define Career Development in the Organization
According to Knowdell, you have to first define what career development is and specify who it is for.

Step 2: Assess the Organization's Need for Career Development
The needs assessment goes from the top (the CEO's perception of need) down through all levels of the organization. As you go through the various levels, you will find that the perceptions of need may vary. Through integration of needs across levels, a pattern of alignment of organizational needs with employee needs will emerge. This leads to the next step in the model.

Step 3: Design a Program for the Organization
The needs assessment process will serve as the basis for the identification of services and delivery methods. At this step, input from benchmarking activities will help to identify the programs of other, similar companies and to identify creative and innovative ways of serving the company and the employees.

Step 4: Promote the Program Internally

Just as the perceptions of needs will vary, so also will the perceptions of career development. Key to the development of a successful program is the communication of the program to all stakeholders and its promotion across organizations and levels within the organizations.

The initial four steps focus on the design and building of the program itself. The assumption here is that the program is managed and located within or through the career center. The remaining steps focus on the delivery of the services within the program and the management of the career development processes.

Step 5: Acknowledge the Individual Employee's Emotions

Changes within the company, the organization, and the specific workplace, create emotional responses across all levels of the organization. Times of change, whether from downsizing or expansion or anything in between, will serve to trigger emotional responses that need to be recognized and resolved.

Step 6: Guide Employee's Assessment Process

If assessment is part of the comprehensive program, and in most cases it should be, the career center staff needs to be expert in the assessments used, as well as in their interpretation and application.

Step 7: Facilitate Employee's Exploration Process

Internal career development may have very limited opportunities available, or may have a wide variety of opportunities, some of which may be hidden. The staff of the corporate career center is responsible to assist and guide the employees in exploring opportunities for development and for job change.

Step 8: Participate in Employee's Goal Setting and Planning

The career center staff will employ a variety of processes, tools, and techniques in assisting the employee to define self and job potential and to identify opportunities and potentials for meaningful employment.

Step 9: Coach Employee in Implementing the Career Strategy

Once an employee has accessed a new job, the work of the career services staff is not finished. Coaching for job success may be a necessary step for some employees, especially in new or difficult types of work. And the career services staff may provide first-line interventions in working with managers, supervisors, or other employees in helping establish an environment in which employees can be successful.

(Knowdell 1996)

Knowdell (1996) makes evident that the ultimate consumers of the program services are employees. All of the other types of career centers are there to deal with customers and clients who use the centers and their services and then go away, either with needs met or in a dissatisfied state. Corporate career centers must meet the needs of the employee in order to meet the needs of the company. And if the needs of the two are not in alignment, then the career centers will soon cease to exist.

BUILDING CAREER DEVELOPMENT CULTURES

One of the unique features of the corporate career center is the opportunity to lead the building of the career development culture within the company. What is a career development culture? First of all, culture is the actions, attitudes, and behaviors that come from the beliefs and values of an organization or a group that uniquely defines the way that they live and interact. A corporation's career development culture is how a company defines itself relative to the actions it takes, the programs it offers, and the attitudes it displays toward the employees at all levels relative to career issues and concepts. Some companies will design and communicate their key beliefs and their core values as foundations for action followed by statements of mission, purpose, initiatives, goals, objectives, and strategies, which will guide the actions to be taken. The relationship of these statements to career development will be reflected in the level and extent to which the employees are recognized or identified within each statement.

The career development culture of a corporation will reflect the degree to which career development is integrated or infused at all levels, across all organizations. To better understand the career development culture in an organization, consider three perspectives: employee career development, organizational development, and corporate development. These three perspectives can be further delineated into three sections: the foundations, drivers, and enablers. Frasier (1995) created a model describing these components.

A company that has a highly defined career development culture will have foundations that spell out beliefs and values and relate them to the beliefs and values of the employees. The employees, in turn, will align their beliefs and values with those of the corporation to build capacity for productivity. The foundations under employee career development include individual values and belief, capacities, and personal commitment. These translate, under corporate development, as corporate values and beliefs, corporate capacities, and leadership commitment (Frasier 1995).

Drivers represent those things from the viewpoint of the employee and the organization that moves performance and productivity forward within the company. The drivers for the employee serve as the road map for alignment with the organization for which they work. These drivers serve to keep the employee on track in meeting the needs of the organization while meeting their own needs. The mutual fulfillment of aligned needs is one way in which corporate career development is unique compared to other career development settings. Drivers related to employee career development are: aspirations, life fulfillment, professional preparation, career planning, training plan and education plans, and individual dedication. When considering the organizational career development perspective, drivers would include: being a premier employer, having a best-in-class workforce, continuous improvement, and 360 degree feedback opportunities. Drivers under corporate development incorporate: the vision, business needs and strategies, the investment in becoming a learning corporation, and policies that respect employees (Frasier 1995). In summary, the drivers identified from the corporate development perspective represent the big picture that encompasses the organizational drivers and serves as the centering point for everything done by employees across the organizations, at all levels. These corporate drivers, like the corporate values and beliefs, reflect the way employees are valued in the career development culture of a company (Frasier 1995).

Enablers identify the processes that are used in all three perspectives. It also identifies tools that are essential to the facilitation of the process. For instance, processes that employees use to maintain their employability and value to the company include periodic self-assessment, continuous updating and development of transferable and transportable skills, ongoing participation in education and training, and active involvement in professional associations and activities.

The enablers of organizations are those processes and tools that facilitate the work of the employees and continuous progression toward achievement of organizational goals and objectives, development and expansion of a readily accessible talent pool, and continuous improvement of work processes, products, and services.

The big picture of corporate enablers provides a universal framework for accomplishment of corporate goals and objectives and ties together the work of organizations and independent employee contributors. The broad scope of the corporate enablers keeps everyone working together toward a common purpose and facilitates cross-organization collaboration. Without this framework, companies may tend to develop egocentric silos that lose the benefit of synergistic contribution to the common good.

When the corporate foundations, drivers, and enablers are an integral part of a corporate career development culture, employees at any level and within any organization will find themselves encouraged to grow and develop toward their potential. This type of culture provides an environment in which employee motivation to perform automatically supports the concepts of continuous improvement and total customer satisfaction.

CORPORATE CAREER CENTERS: CHANGES TO THE PRESENT

Corporations that build a career development culture facilitate the development of programs, processes, and services to meet the needs of the employees. There are a variety of processes and tools for doing this. A key tool is the career center.

Corporate career centers developed in the model of other types of centers and tended to provide many of the same services and resources found in noncorporate settings. The key differences were that services and resources were also provided for career development within the company with the eye on retention of the workforce, consistent with the needs of the company.

The three career centers identified earlier have continued to evolve and redefine processes and services. The career center at Eli Lilly has moved from an on-ground service center concept to the virtual center concept. Keys to this transformation included developing online resource access, redefining shared responsibilities of the employees and supervisors, and training supervisors to actively facilitate employee development.

The virtual career center is and will continue to be vital to corporate settings that have become increasingly cost conscious and willing to reduce head count within human resources organizations. The virtual career center has many advantages, including accessibility twenty-four hours a day, seven days a week, links to a wide variety of resources, and immediate access to information. Disadvantages are the loss of personal contact.

LOOKING TO THE FUTURE

The virtual career center will become more and more prevalent with some return to personal contact. Internet options have expanded within the last year or two. Yahoo and other companies offer opportunities to form discussion groups. MySpace and the hosts of Web logs provide opportunities for posting materials and information.

The rapid escalation of distance learning and e-learning modalities makes it possible to offer almost any non-laboratory class online. The development of high-speed Internet and broadband technologies makes it possible to offer visual materials and information with Web cam technology.

The proliferation of wireless handheld devices such as cell phones, Ipods, MP3s, Blackberries, digital cameras, and Palm Pilots will become central to the delivery and exchange of career development-related products and services.

The technologies provided by the computer with an attached camera and sound system make it possible to unite "high-touch" with "high-tech" on an easily accessible basis. With wireless digital technologies in portable computers of many sizes, counseling on-the-go is possible. Include the camera with the portable package, and the high-touch processes can take place in multiple environments and locations.

Voice recognition software has been used for a long time in telephone menus and in the automated answering systems of businesses. The same technology can be applied with "smart technologies" to simulate counseling/advisement sessions, if an adequate database has been developed to provide "smart" alternatives for the requestor.

In 2000, Texas Instruments offered a voice translation software through which English and four other languages could be used for multilingual interactions. Equipment is currently on the market that can translate in many languages. With cameras and this translation software system in place, the virtual career center can easily move to many of the primary national locations of corporate customers and employees.

SUMMARY

Corporate career centers developed out of the need to provide programs and services for employees of companies that were concerned about the welfare of their employees. Typically, such development took place to meet the needs of major changes in businesses relative to downsizing, layoffs, and redeployment of resources. However, as companies became aware of the advantages of building flexible, skilled, and motivated workforces, the emphasis moved to proactive workforce development.

Initially, corporate career centers seemed to adapt the model of established career centers in colleges and employment services. However, with the recognition of the unique nature of the businesses and the desirability of aligning employee needs with company needs, career centers began to evolve. Now the focus is on the employee as a valued human asset. Training is provided to enhance the skills and employability of the employees to meet the performance and production needs of the business.

Traditional career center programs and services continue in many centers with movements of delivery to an Internet and/or intranet base. Distance learning approaches and the shift from on-ground delivery of career services to electronic delivery through a virtual center concept will become more and more prevalent. Adaptation and use of new hardware and software technologies will totally change the face of career processes and services delivery within the corporate career center concept.

The world is coming closer together through technology and the potential use of visual and voice contact, real or virtual.

CHAPTER 11

Partnering with Employers to Offer Career Development and Planning Services

By Pat Fessenden, Sybil Pressprich, and Becky Ryan

Alargely untapped area of growth for career centers is partnering with employers in the community to offer career development and planning programs. These programs can build partnerships, yield revenue, and increase the number of adult participants. The goal of this work is to serve people in the community, build long-term relationships, and invite increased contacts with the career centers.

There are 8,000 baby boomers turning 60 every day (Magali, 2006). Consider the impact this is having on workplace turnover, and this trend is just beginning to hit its stride. The new corporate emphasis is on succession planning as a continual, ongoing process that recognizes the value of strategically planning to have the right person for the right job, as well as identifying up-and-coming talent. Additionally, it is a proactive approach to accommodating a diminishing pool of employees. Historically, such investments in the human component have been hard to measure, and employers must go through a rigorous process to establish standards of comparison for assessment purposes. Employers are more recently discovering the cost benefits associated with life/work initiatives and retaining employees. High turnover can lead to increased expenditures and missed productivity. More employers are working on succession planning to create an environment that encourages retention and looks ahead to companies' long-term personnel needs.

One way that employers can accommodate this trend is to offer opportunities for employees to reassess their skills, develop clear goals, and maximize their strengths. Despite the value placed on career planning, individuals seeking career growth can meet resistance due to dwindling budgets and shrinking human resource departments. Human resource departments are struggling to offer career development and planning services to employees. This pressure has made them more open to creating new partnerships with career centers on a contract basis. The opportunity for a career center to fill this niche in this new marketplace holds much promise.

At the same time, career centers are faced with the challenge of streamlining budgets and managing expenditures. Career centers and employers can benefit by working together. To achieve this, career centers need to understand and apply corporate terminology and practices from an educational environment to bridge the long-standing gaps between these two worlds.

The concept and practice of career development and planning has been in existence in education for years, and now, in a fast-paced economic time, educators have information to share. While career experts are not unfamiliar with consulting and contracting with constituencies outside of education, career centers are recent arrivals on the scene. Although many career centers offer a wide variety of informational and free programs for community members, providing fee-based services requires a shift in mindset as well as thoughtful planning and marketing.

As career centers consider this prospect, it is important to begin by reviewing the career center's core mission. Each career center has its own unique process for contracting and working with outside constituencies. It is important to understand how career center policies and procedures interact with employer's policies and procedures.

MUTUAL BENEFITS

For those organizations that choose to work with career centers, there are many benefits, including

- assisting employees with the development of career plans
- providing the tools needed for employees to accept responsibility for their own career progression
- becoming an organization that offers on-site career development with the goal of higher employee satisfaction, improved employee retention, and increased productivity
- promoting career development workshops that can add to team-building experiences as employees discover different strengths and complementary goals
- linking professional development and continuing education to career development, which creates a continuous learning organization leading to better educated employees
- working to promote employee retention and succession planning for long-term personnel needs that reflect the overall goals of the organization
- subcontracting career development for an overloaded human resources office, whose staff may not be trained or have the time to provide career development
- providing employees with up-to-date skills and career plans, which gives them confidence in their ability to master any transition, particularly if they face downsizing or significant workplace changes.

Additionally, there are benefits for career centers seeking these partnerships with employers. Employers who turn to a career center for workshops may well return to ask about course development, other workshops, and other services. Career centers can gain

- a clearer understanding of what employers seek, with an eye toward improved placement of graduates

- a better sense of workplace issues, leading to better preparation of students, adults, and clients
- ongoing revision of workshops, keeping the career center on the cutting edge in the employment world
- a sense of accessibility and openness for adults seeking additional education
- a source of revenue.

FUNDAMENTAL CONSIDERATIONS TO ADDRESS

Several challenges exist in making the venture into these new partnerships. Foremost among these is making a distinction between the role and mission of a career center and the role and mission of a private outplacement/career development firm. Career centers should begin this process with the mission, vision, and goals close in hand, to keep the perspective grounded, and the potential for exploring possible roles enhanced.

An essential first step is to become familiar with the needs of employers in the area. Often, initial requests come from local government agencies and service industries, where employers have little time to help employees with career planning and development, but wanted assistance with retaining hard-working employees who are eager to grow in their responsibilities and take on new challenges. An environmental scan or survey can clarify the needs of organizations and employers. A critical question is "what employers in your area need most as it relates to career development and planning." This initial assessment must be accompanied by a review of who the local providers are, as well their areas of expertise. A review of local providers of career services listed in the phone book can be followed by informational interviews with pertinent organizational members. Focus groups, surveys, or a series of coordinated conversations with targeted employers are examples of specific starting points. A beneficial by-product to this work can be the cultivation of productive working relationships with colleagues in the private sector and listening carefully to their ideas.

A critical next step is to identify the services best suited for the career center to provide. Begin by creating a list of programs and workshops that could be expanded to serve a new audience. This is also an opportunity to assess the areas of expertise among career center staff members and to consider what programs are already offered by others in your market. Be sure to investigate state job service agencies, private career counselors, and colleagues in the field. Also review the types of services and support offered by online career coaching/mentoring providers. Investigating the market, accompanied by thoughtful strategic planning, can lead to center success. It is far better be proactive to avoid costly errors later.

NEXT, TIME TO START

Following a thorough review, it's time to make decisions about what selected programs the center might want to offer at the workplace. Start with one or two pilot programs at little or no cost and invite extensive feedback. Midcourse corrections are key factors for building a successful program.

Employers may request services outside of career development, such as organizational development. It is better to refer these requests to more qualified providers. Knowing who the local providers are for a wide variety of organizational consulting issues can help aid in making a connection for the employer and will encourage the focus to remain on the career center's expertise. If the initial research was done well, the career center will be rewarded with a solid foundation for appropriate referrals.

In many situations the contact will be with the company's human resources department. Establishing an effective working relationship is important as roles and responsibilities, and work requirements are negotiated. Career development practitioners generally deal with the individual and his or her goals and aspirations. However, if the organization is contracting for services, it may become challenging to balance the organizational goals with those of the individual. Having ongoing conversations with the human resources representative, including an agreement about the confidentiality of conversations with employees, is critical to success. In addition, gathering information from the organization about workplace climate and culture, as well as clarifying organizational expectations, is an essential element in working effectively with employees.

MARKETING YOUR SERVICES TO EMPLOYERS

First, identify interested employers and specify the exact services you will offer by

- identifying the client you serve, whether it is the organization or the individual
- identifying the organization's needs through individual conversations with key organizational contacts
- clarifying what services you will deliver and what is better contracted with another provider
- becoming familiar with workplace culture and expectations
- explaining how career development can help retain experienced employees and assist the company in succession planning for future needs
- maintaining confidentiality in a competitive employment environment and confirming that with the employer client
- sharing evaluation comments with the employers and encouraging them to take key comments to heart and consider making changes in key programs and services.

Developing a clear plan to market your services may require partnering with other program providers or services. Ideally, connecting with an office or program provider that has experience marketing programs increases the chances of using strategies that work.

It is also helpful to seek and use resources outside of the career center for getting the word out and marketing services. These may include attending or presenting at professional association meetings such as the Society of Human Resource Managers (SHRM) or the American Society for Training and Development (ASTD). Using these opportunities to connect with and inform human resource professionals about services builds the initial relationships with employers.

A large part of marketing has to do with pricing. The environmental scan of what is currently available in the community can yield information about prices. Questions to ask include: What are other career services and private agencies charging for workshops and services in your area? Do they use package rates, à la carte options, percentage discounts, and guarantees? Does the career center mission include providing services free or low cost for area employers, and what impact will this have on pricing your workshops?

After the success of initial programs in this new market, employer clients became the best marketers for our career center and often referred colleagues from their own agencies and professional associations to us.

TYPES OF SERVICES

Although your research will provide guidance for the types of services you may want to offer, seeking input from the employer on a case-by-case basis is a critical step to ensure you are addressing the needs of your audience. Employers may need help in clarifying their goals and desired outcomes, and you may need to ask many questions before clearly understanding what their needs are. This process will help in tailoring your offerings to the consumers. Services can include

- outplacement services, ranging from individual appointments to small-group career workshops focused on retooling
- career development workshops that help employees identify how they might grow within an organization

- preretirement planning workshops that encourage employees to consider post retirement activities and goals
- educational planning sessions in which employees are acquainted with opportunities for continuing education and have the opportunity to have questions answered by knowledgeable people from the learning institution
- training for human resources personnel to improve their skills in facilitating career planning activities
- consulting with organizations to help design career development programs that they then implement.

SELECTED WORKSHOPS TO MEET EMPLOYERS' NEEDS

Myers Briggs Type Indicator (MBTI)

The MBTI is a widely used and respected personality assessment. It provides insights to improve communication, decision-making, problem-solving, and interpersonal skills and can be used in many settings, including career development, team building, and leadership training. Organizations find the MBTI attractive because of its multiple uses. This workshop is often requested by employers. One challenge of the MBTI is that only qualified people are able to access it and to effectively interpret the results. The interpretation session usually takes approximately three hours, with application to a specific area taking longer. Some employers may find this time investment too long. At the same time, the MBTI can be very helpful for employees to gain a better understanding of their job satisfaction and to improve interpersonal skills with a work group. For more information about the MBTI, contact the Association for Psychological Type International at http://www.aptinternational. org/ or CPP (formerly Consulting Psychologist Press) at http://www.cpp.com/.

The Strong Interest Inventory

Career centers have also had some success using the Strong Interest Inventory with employers as part of their management training program. Strong is a vocational-interest assessment and can be used to help employees who are considering a management role to clarify areas of interest. Similar to the MBTI, Strong requires training to administer and interpret. In addition, it is important to use these assessments with caution to ensure that they are not used to inappropriately dictate an individual's career path.

The Job Search Process

This encompasses a variety of topics delivered in either a series of shorter sessions or a longer comprehensive workshop. These sessions are designed to assist participants in developing an effective job search. Topics include networking, interviewing, and writing résumés and cover letters. Assistance in targeting future employers could also be provided. Approximately four to six hours are needed to address these topics, depending on how in-depth they are covered and how many topics are covered. In addition to addressing the tools of a job search, most job seekers need ongoing resources and assistance. Weekly job search support groups that address managing stress, dealing with rejection and depression, and staying engaged in the job search process have also been found to be successful.

Offering job search services may lead you into the outplacement services area, which comes with its own set of challenges. These may include dealing with newly released employees, who may be angry, confused, and reluctant to begin a job search. This may be a departure from the typical client seen in a career center. It may be helpful to connect with outplacement providers to gain a better understanding of these services and how best to assist these individual.

Surviving Unemployment

Discussion in this session focuses on coping with change, confusion, and other frustrations of unemployment. Participants are assisted with developing a plan to help them cope with this difficult time of transition. Partnering with professionals from the human resources and employee assistance departments on campus, at your local state job center office, or at the contracting employer can help strengthen this workshop,. which could be one to three hours long.

Coping with Change in Your Career

This workshop helps participants identify the emotions associated with change. Methods for coping with the uncertainty and stress of change are discussed, as well as goal setting and focusing on change as a positive part of life. This topic adapts well to a presentation at career fairs and is one to two hours in length.

Tools for Career Planning

This is a comprehensive workshop that teaches the process of career planning and decision making. Participants engage in self-assessment by identifying their skills, values, interests, and personal preferences and use this information to develop a career plan. The Strong Interest Inventory and the Myers Briggs Type Indicator (MBTI) are completed before the workshop, and participants receive their results during the workshop. In addition to these standardized assessments, skills and values card-sort activities are also used. A panel of people who have completed a career change discuss the challenges they faced and career change success tips. Time is spent on resources for career planning. These include Web-based resources, books, and informational interviewing. Participants develop specific career goals and begin development of a career plan. This workshop takes approximately sixteen hours and is done on two consecutive days. Its challenges include the length of the workshop and the need to be trained and qualified to administer and interpret the MBTI and the Strong Interest Inventory.

Other services and programs career centers can offer employers include the following:

- a listserve for adults retooling and thinking about returning to school, which allows prospective and returning adult students to network online and share survival tips for those busy first months

- layoff or nonrenewal transition workshops for employers in the community
- online career workshops geared for busy working professionals
- educational fairs, including educational information sessions, offered with area educational institutions at employers' workplaces
- individual counseling appointments, with evening appointments and free parking available
- partnerships with human resource professionals to deliver programs they design, and assisting them in growing their in-house career development program
- returning-to-school informational and advising programs, open to newly enrolled or prospective students to help demystify the process of taking that first step back into education after significant time away
- one-stop portal access for employers to tap into nearby educational institutions' wealth of services and programs
- development of a consortia to offer employers one-call service—i.e., calling any of the member centers to set up an educational fair, informational program, or career workshop; one example of this is the Southern Wisconsin Association for Continuing Higher Education, found at http://www.swache.org.

USEFUL WEB SITES

The following Web sites provide additional information relating to this chapter's topics.

Organizations that can conduct an environmental scan of your area to see what services already exist and what may be needed:

- Society for Human Resource Management (SHRM) is at http://www.shrm.org/
- American Society for Training and Development (ASTD) is at http://www.astd.org/astd

Helpful Web sites for information about skills assessments and workshop ideas:

- http://www.acinet.org/acinet/skills/default.aspx
- http://www.rileyguide.com/assess.html#skills
- http://www.iseek.org/sv/index.jsp

Career center Web site information from the University of Wisconsin-Madison Adult and Student Services Center:

- http://www.dcs.wisc.edu/services/career.htm
- http://www.dcs.wisc.edu/services/outreach.htm

SUMMARY

The role of career centers is changing. Partnering with employers can be an exciting new venture. Succession planning, employee development, retirement planning, and similar movements are happening across a multitude of corporate, nonprofit, and academic environments. Career centers can use their expertise in career development and their knowledge of the job market to be at the cutting edge. As career centers work to share the message that supporting employee development is an important social value, it also pushes out the boundaries of education and shares expertise with the community in new ways. In addition, offering unbiased, solid expertise, at a reasonable cost and in a straightforward, easy to understand format holds captivating promise. A thorough review of the center's mission and vision, followed by a comprehensive exploration and increased familiarity with the needs of the community will place the career center in a solid vantage point from which to operate.

CHAPTER 12

Career Centers
on the Internet

by Donald A. Schutt Jr.

Career centers take a number of different forms on the Internet. Virtual career centers, by definition, exist only on the Internet. This is the case for many of the centers that offer services online, but it is also the case that existing career centers in physical locations are developing Web interfaces to extend their services well beyond their geographic and time limitations. This provides exciting opportunities for connecting career center users with vital and bountiful information on the Internet, but it should be approached with caution. As the number of Web sites offering career development assistance increases, so does the possibility that users will be mislead, misinformed, or charged for services that may be neither comprehensive nor useful. Accepting both the positive and negative possibilities, this chapter considers the development, implementation, and management of an online career center. Several sites that deliver career-related information and services are highlighted as are some emerging technologies to watch.

At one point in time, locating and accessing career and labor market information was the primary challenge facing those considering their career development. The Internet is proving to be a useful solution to that problem; now, the challenge has become synthesizing the plethora of information into a manageable and personally meaningful career plan. Sampson (1997) proposed that the Internet could serve four specific functions for its users:

1. "Identify problems and possibilities by using links to surf among Internet sites to discover the range of data that is available, e.g., surfing serendipity.
2. Search for information to solve a problem by using a search engine or an Internet site.
3. Obtain information when users know what they want by accessing a specific Internet site or by using a search engine to link to a specific Internet site address.
4. Communicate with others via email, file transfer, chat mode, and eventually videoconferencing."

The Internet is used in many different ways to deliver career development. Some Web sites serve specific populations such as the American Chemical Society's (ACS) employment resources site (http://www.chemistry.org/portal/a/c/s/1/career.html?DOC=careers\index.html). ACS delivers articles, salary comparison tools, and access to career coaching via the Web.

With so much information and so many sites, how can the Internet be used effectively for career development? Sampson (1997) suggested that the Internet should not be used in isolation from other career development resources, but in conjunction with them. Similarly, it is important to combine Internet use with periods of reflection and of interaction with others. Sampson (1997) also suggested that the Internet be used primarily for networking and gathering information, while bearing in mind that users must be directed to the Web sites that are most appropriate for their individual needs. Pyle (2006) was more specific: "The counselor needs the computer for its wealth of information but the client needs the counselor to make sense of and to shape a direction that fully utilizes the information generated." In addition, Pyle identified five competency areas for counselors using computers:

1. The counselor is well-versed and knowledgeable of valid and reliable technology driven career information systems/programs either in the form of computer-assisted guidance and/or Internet sites.
2. The counselor effectively diagnoses the client's career development need. The counselor will need to be sure that the presenting issue/need has been accurately evaluated.
3. The counselor motivates the client's involvement in the technology source.
4. The counselor processes information generated from the technology source.
5. The counselor helps the client to shape helpful steps. The counselor is interested in an action plan that will be implemented beyond the life of the counseling experience. (Pyle 2006)

Further consideration has been given to the delivery of career information and planning services as well as Webcounseling services. The National Career Development Association addressed these issues in the "Guidelines for the Use of the Internet for Provision of Career Information and Planning Services" (www. ncda.org listed under the "Internet Resources"). NCDA is currently reviewing the ethical guidelines with a revision due out in 2007. In the draft version of that revision, the role of counseling and the use of the Internet are further defined. Under the same listing on the NCDA site is the resource "Internet Sites for Career Planning." Similarly, the National Board for Certified Counselors, Inc. has also "The Practice of Internet Counseling" (http://www. nbcc.org/ethics2).

PLANNING A WEB SITE

When planning a Web site, there are some basic questions that need to be addressed:

- What is your purpose?
- Who are you trying to reach?
- Who are your competitors and how will you differ from them?
- What resources do you have for set-up and maintenance?
- What are your expectations of success?
- How will you measure success?

(Based on Tauber and Kienan 1997)

These questions are similar to questions asked in the planning stages for physical career centers. The most important step is deciding on a clear purpose for the site and developing the structure and content on paper prior to putting the Web site together. Often, sites are developed "on-the-fly" and lack consistent graphical themes, send users in information loops that never end, and ultimately lose users due to poor planning. To prevent this from occurring, create a flow chart that follows each step a user would experience as they move about your site.

In deciding how Web pages should be arranged, it is best to aim for something between the extremes of a dull, book-like format and an overwhelming excess of graphics and hypermedia. The first approach clearly does not take proper advantage of hyperlinks and similar features that make Internet use so quick, easy, and enjoyable. The second approach has the unpleasant effect of showing off exciting features at the expense of simple navigation and even of substantial information. Two examples of organizational techniques that can be employed include a hierarchical approach and multiple tracks for multiple audiences. The hierarchical approach follows an outline with the ability to build as many levels as needed. If the pages are accessed by individuals with different levels of experience in either the content or the process, it may be worthwhile to consider a multiple path approach.

The CareerInfoNet (http://www.careernet.org) Web site exemplifies the multiple path approach for different audiences. Developed as a cooperative effort by educational institutions, businesses, and government, it provides students and job seekers in the community of West Bend and Washington County, Wisconsin, with an integrated and dynamic source of electronic information about career information and opportunities. Users are able to access the site from one of the official locations including middle schools, high schools, colleges, public libraries, and the local workforce development center or from any computer with an Internet connection. The career information on the site is drawn from local, state, and national sources and is continually updated.

When planning the center's Web site, consider these tips from Tauber and Kienan (1997) for creating smashing Web pages:

- Give your site a title that's brief, descriptive, and easy to remember.
- Keep the title's promise, and provide all content you say you will.
- At the top of each page, offer clues about what's on the page. Don't assume that people are going to scroll unless you give them a reason to scroll. Break pages that are more than three screenfuls long into multiple pages.
- Make anything that looks like a button act like a button.
- Make links meaningful—avoid generic "Click Here" links, and decide whether you're going to link on the active phrase ("Go To") or the destination phrase ("Our Chat Archive").
- Use small image files that contain no more than 50 colors.
- Keep directory names and filenames short and consistent.
- Tell your users the size of any downloadable files—they need to know whether they can manage a file of this size.
- Provide an e-mail link to the Webmaster.
- Before you announce the site, test it until you can't stand to test it anymore. Get others to test it. Find all the bugs and squash them. Then launch.

MANAGING THE ONLINE CAREER CENTER

One of the most fundamental choices in regard to managing the online career center is whether you will host the site yourself or use an Internet service provider (ISP). If the former, you must thoroughly research the amount of resources—time, money, staff—involved in such a task, as these can be considerable. If the latter, you must still make provision for paying and interfacing with the ISP. Your university, school district, or company may already have Internet services or connections that you can take advantage of, so it is best to examine this possibility before taking any action.

Staffing

Staffing the Web presence is an important task that often requires many different individuals. Internet-related job titles can be confusing and job descriptions often change with the technology, but most Web sites require workers in the following roles: Webmasters, Web developers, network systems administrators, programmers, and customer service representatives. A career center hosting its own large site might require more than one person in each role, whereas smaller sites might have just one or two people filling all of these positions. A career center using an ISP may only have a part-time Webmaster on staff to communicate ideas, changes, and problems to the ISP.

Briefly, the *Webmaster* is, as the term implies, the authority on what goes into the Web site, when it goes in, how it will look, and all the other concerns of starting and maintaining the site. Nevertheless, the Webmaster of a university or corporation Web site, for example, may ultimately have to answer to a higher authority such as a dean or vice president. Tauber and Kienan (1997) described four types of Webmasters: the tech Webmaster with hardcore technical skills, the content Webmaster well-versed in creating content, the production Webmaster handling everything from design to scanning art, and the executive Webmaster with perhaps no Web experience but plenty of project management expertise.

Web developers (also called *designers* or *publishers*) are "responsible for the actual creation of the Web site. After collaborating with the Webmaster to lay out the conceptual framework of the site and establish performance constraints, the developer begins the day-to-day activities necessary to design the Web pages" (Steinberg 1997).

Network systems administrators keep the network's computers up and running. Responsible for facilitating the links between servers and Internet providers, they might also monitor network traffic.

Programmers essentially implement the ideas of Webmasters or Web developers, though they may be one and the same person. They write instructions for computers using Hypertext Markup Language (HTML), which tells browsers how to display each page. Programmers frequently customize existing or off-the-shelf software to meet specific needs.

Customer service representatives offer business or technical support, usually on behalf of Internet service providers. Only those career centers hosting their own sites are likely to have customer service representatives, but these representatives often provide necessary assistance when a site is not operating properly.

There are currently Internet content management systems that provide opportunities for non-IT staff to work directly to deliver Web page content to the Internet. One example is DotNetNuke (www.dotnetnuke.com), an open-source Web Application Framework ideal for creating and implementing web sites, corporate intranets and extranets, online publishing portals, and custom application. It is open-source software which is available at no cost. It is built on a Microsoft ASP.NET platform and is easily installed and hosted. DotNetNuke is one of many existing and emerging technology innovations that are changing the nature of moving content to the Web.

The Web Site Budget

Consider three different expense classes when developing Web site budgets: infrastructure, production, and ongoing support. Again, there will be appreciable differences between budgets for career centers hosting their own sites and those that use ISPs. *Infrastructure* encompasses all of the tangible items needed to construct and maintain a site, from office space and computers to an Internet connection and related telephone bills. *Production* costs include everything involved in getting the site up and running, such as design and programming expenses. *Ongoing support* usually involves paying people to regularly update the site or add new materials to it as needed. It can be tempting to cut costs by reducing this part of the budget, but Web sites lose their attraction and usefulness if they are not kept up-to-date. If you are unwilling or unable to maintain the site as you should, it might be best to reevaluate your plans to go online.

Measuring Success

Planning for evaluation is as important for Web sites as it is for other aspects of the career center. Often, measuring success on the Internet is a challenging endeavor for many reasons. One is that defining success is difficult enough without the complicating factor of technology. Another is that technology factor itself: what information is gathered and how that indicates success. The following summary provides suggestions for measuring the success of Web pages:

- Hits, impressions, and traffic reports: Hits are the number of files that are accessed on your Website. A hit is generated for every page of text and every graphic or video file. A single page may generate a number of hits. Impressions occur each time a single page on your site is loaded. It is a much better indicator of popularity but more difficult to measure. Traffic counts the number of visits that have occurred in a discrete time frame. The challenge in counting traffic is deciding how to measure it. If you can figure that part out, you can gather valuable data about your Web use.
- Media presence: How much media attention do you receive? Even a mention in the local paper can indicate that your

site is generating interest. Another method of measuring the popularity of your site is to count the backlinks—or the links on other sites that go to your site.

- Information gathered and reported: Perhaps understanding the center's target population more thoroughly is success in itself. You can gather data while also gaining an understanding of how popular your site is.
- Subject responses: If users mention the site, perhaps in responses to the Webmaster from the email prompt, consider this subjective data as useful as other measures of success.

(Condensed from Tauber and Kienan 1997)

EXAMPLES

There are a number of career center sites worth visiting on the Internet to sample a variety of methods of delivering career information.

- ALMIS State Occupational Projections: http://www. doleta.gov/almis/map.cfm
- America's Job Bank, featuring search tips along with job market information, employers and job seekers sites, and job market information: http://www.ajb.dni.us/
- Florida State University Career Center providing services for a number of different groups: http://www.career.fsu.edu
- Monster Board Career Center with Resume Builder, career resources, career advice, relocating services, and other links: http://content.monster.com

One challenge facing career centers attempting to provide career services on the Internet is how to teach the process of career development and then support that process. Most of the sites listed here (and in the majority of career-related Internet books) offer pieces that support the career development process but do not teach or support the whole process. That process, once again, consists of answering three questions: Who am I?, Where am I going?, and How do I get there? Many of the career-related sites are helpful to users making a transition from one situation to another, but few of the sites focus on a lifelong process of developing career maturity and making lifelong, personally meaningful plans.

There is one notable exception that is moving in the direction necessary to provide more comprehensive career planning and development services on the Internet. Connected to Bowling Green State University (http://www.bgsu.edu/office/sa/career/students/page17957.html), this site is titled "Major Career Planning." The site provides basic information on the process of career development along with some helpful beginning activities and information. The challenge is providing the expertise necessary to guide an individual through the career development process. While this site offers a different approach than the great majority of sites, more work needs to be done before it can replicate the expertise available at career center at a physical location.

CAREER CENTERS AND EMERGING TECHNOLOGY

There are too many technological advances to try to effectively provide an overview but these three are samples of the existing and innovative advances that may change the delivery of career services in the future.

1. Podcasting as a strategy for delivering content, primarily multimedia, to vast audiences via mobile devices and computers. If you could imagine the best "interviewing tips" workshop offered by your career center being saved and provided as a download that is then used as an interview preparation tool as an adult jobseeker is walking to her interview. Follow this trend at http://www.podcast.net.

2. Skype (http://www.skype.com), is a program for making calls to anyone else in the world who also has Skype and,

at the time of the printing, was available to download at no cost. It can also call landlines and mobile phones. Skype was recently purchased by eBay for use as a communication tool to connect people throughout the world. Imagine your career center connecting a current college student in Nebraska to an alumni/mentor in India and have them talk monthly for an hour at no cost. Skype promises to be a great interpersonal connectivity tool that could be used effectively and at no or a low cost.

3. Adobe Acrobat Connect Professional (http://www.adobe.com/products/acrobatconnectpro/) provides online meeting and online interaction support and, when combined with Adobe Connect Training and Adobe Presenter, a number of innovative possibilities are within reach. An example, tools like Connect Professional could allow a veteran in one location to have his resume interactively reviewed by an expert at a different location. Career Centers can collaborate, communicate, and teach online from the comfort of a central location.

4. Mediasite by Sonic Foundry (http://www.mediasite.com/) makes Webcasting easy. It allows an immediate visual and audio capture of events like presentations and classes and almost immediately posts them to a searchable Web site. Even if the technology is not used, the Web site search tool provides access to a large library of topics. One example is a "Dress for Success" workshop that is available at http://www.mediasite.com/presentation.aspx?p=1796. This topic might be a useful add-on to an interviewing workshop. The combination of Powerpoint, audio and video provide user with access to unlimited possibilities.

5. Moodle (http://moodle.org/) is free, open source, online courseware to assist you in developing career development courses that can be shared via the Web. It also provides support and resources for expanding to create online learning communities.

One example for new opportunities in the way that career centers approach the Internet is the increasing need for individuals to develop an online identity including a Web portfolio. While this area is still emerging and may not be necessary for every job seeker, it is still critical for career centers to consider how to meet the online needs of customers and to move beyond collecting and synthesizing information to taking control of the information and helping career center users to become creators of content. One very useful Web log that discusses this in detail is http://blog.brandego.com.

SUMMARY

Career centers on the Internet may serve a variety of purposes and users, including

- replicating the services of a physical career center for those unable to reach it,
- supplementing the basic services of a physical career center,
- assisting only a specific population (i.e., medical students, displaced workers),
- acting as a clearinghouse for other career-related sites, and
- actually taking the place of a physical career center.

As you proceed with your online career center, bear in mind that the medium of the Internet has its pitfalls as well as exciting possibilities. While accessing masses of job listings or blithely following link after link, users can easily be distracted from the entire process of career development. With careful planning and informed usage, however, career centers online can be a worthwhile and innovative addition to the career development process.

CHAPTER 13

Planning for Action

by Donald A. Schutt Jr.

This action plan is intended to serve as a road map for the processes described in the preceding chapters. Any good planning process recognizes that three factors often determine success. First, it is necessary to set goals to achieve goals. Second, writing goals down and reviewing them often increases the chances of meeting those goals. Finally, if the goals involve groups of people (a group defined here simply as more than one person), it is important to have a level of agreement within the group relative to the goals. Goal setting is sometimes viewed as an arduous task because it is important to not only build into the plan the strategies for evaluation, but also to adhere to that plan. Recognizing growth and progress toward goals can reinvigorate, decrease the burden that evaluation seems to be, and offer an opportunity for reflection and, one hopes, celebration, as the career center succeeds.

This chapter discusses preplanning activities as well as action planning. The level of detail in this action plan has been minimized so that a broader planning picture surfaces. Each of the components of the action plan has been discussed in the planning and development chapters or demonstrated in the chapters depicting career centers in action.

PREPLANNING ACTIVITIES

Identify who will initially lead the development of the career center.

✔ Choose an individual or group capable of succeeding in developing the career center.

✔ Identify a person or a group with
- a working knowledge of career development;
- the authority or access to the authority necessary to make decisions;
- collaborative relationships with key potential partners;
- the capability to effectively and efficiently facilitate a task-oriented work group through the completion of a large-scale project;
- the creativity necessary to navigate complex challenges;
- access to relevant individual, community, or organizational information; and
- the respect of those in the community or organization.

Depending on the scope of the project, it might be valuable to identify a project manager. The need for project management expertise may range from occasional consulting or advising to employing a full-time project manager for the start-up phase to help

- develop an overall structure and strategy for managing the start-up process;
- identify all of the required and desired start-up tasks;
- organize the tasks and develop a schedule based on anticipate duration;

- identify the optimum configuration of available human resources to complete the tasks;
- develop processes to identify and mitigate risks, develop a communication plan, track progress toward goals, and develop status reports to monitor the budget, schedule, quality, and scope of the work.

Also important to the project in preplanning is the creation of a Project Charter, which could be used for larger projects (like developing a career center) or smaller projects (like improving a Web site). A charter is typically captured on a document with the following elements: Project title, date/charter version, project name, project manager, primary stakeholder (who is this important to), sponsor(s) or the person or people who have asked for the project to be done or are paying for the project, project description, business case/ statement of need, customers and their need requirements, project definition (including project primary and secondary goals, the scope of the project and any project assumptions), project constraints, project milestones, communication plan, change management procedures, project management team (divided into members, roles and responsibilities), a list of the stakeholders, and most importantly a sign-off section for the sponsors, resource managers, and anyone else critical to be in the information loop. Charters are a very useful tool for keeping the goals of the project in focus (reducing scope-creep), reminding those asking for the project of the needed resources including time, and for the project manager to mark the milestones and accomplishments on the way to achieving the desired outcome.

Set the Stage

✔ Build the career center on a sound conceptual foundation comprising
  - clear career-related definitions;
  - understandable, user-friendly processes (answering the three questions);

- access for all potential users;
- resources to broaden or reinforce users' self-knowledge and understanding;
- strategies to increase individual users' capacity for managing virtually limitless information; and
- an endorsement for the inclusion of education, work, family, cultural, and economic factors/issues in lifelong personal career development plans.

✔ Recognize that the ultimate goal of the career center activities is to empower individuals to become the architects of their career development.

✔ As an organization, embrace and advocate for the subtle yet significant shift from a transition or placement focus to an individual lifelong career development focus. If the career center is intended to be transition- or placement-focused (as some might), be sure to identify to users the specific role in the career development process that your center is addressing with support and services.

ACTION PLANNING

Step One: Define Concerns, Challenges, and Needs

✔ Plan a needs assessment that identifies both individual and community needs—the goal is to compare what is already in existence with what needs to be provided.

- Collect data to substantiate or challenge previous findings or assumptions.
- Identify individual, organizational, and community needs, concerns, and challenges.
- One example of a community need or challenge might be meeting the needs of serving individuals in multiple languages. The Department of Justice identified strategies that organizations used to cre-

ate a coherent plan for communicating with Limited-English-Proficient (LEP) individuals:
A. Determine your organization's language service needs;
B. Identify language resources to help you meet those needs, and ensure that personnel know how to access and effectively use those resources;
C. Familiarize and train staff and managers with effective and innovative methods of communication with LEP individuals;
D. Implement and enforce quality control measures to ensure that you are communicating accurately and effectively with LEP community members; and
E. Conduct outreach to ensure that all community members, regardless of national origin or language, know that they can access your program, and can provide feedback to you on the language services you provide (Condensed from U.S. Department of Justice "Let Everyone Participate" Web site http://www.lep.gov/lepdoc%20chapter1.htm retrieved November 12, 2006)

- Determine why this is a concern, challenge, or need.

✔ Determine what other information is needed to make a good decision when addressing this challenge.

✔ Prioritize the issues by importance, if possible; you might find that some concerns are symptomatic of a more intense challenge.

✔ Translate to goals (or more broadly into mission or purpose).

✔ If the career center does not have explicit and articulated mission, vision, values or principles of practice, and strategies/priorities, the delineation of these might be the best place to begin.

Step Two: Seek Solutions

✔ Review the goals.
- Address the goals with the easiest solutions.
- Identify the challenges demanding more complex solutions.
- Reevaluate the priorities.

✔ Identify indicators of success.
- Define measures of success gathered through formative evaluation.
- Similarly, define measures of overall programmatic (summative) success.

✔ Determine what will prevent you from succeeding.
- Respond with creative solutions to obstacles.
- Re-evaluate the obstacles relative to the importance of the goal.

✔ Connect solutions to resources (including staff and materials).
- Choose an advisory group.
- Plan for recruiting and hiring staff.
- Identify resources.
- Assessment tools.
- Career and labor market information.
- Strategy-based references.
- Create a plan for choosing a location.

✔ Develop a budget connected to resources that are in turn connected to solutions.

✔ Mapping your strategies (or solutions) can help to better understand the interaction between the career center's goals and plan for success. To do this, consider at your strategies from four perspectives: the career center user's perspective, from an internal processes perspective, from a staff learning and growth perspective, and from the financial perspective (Kaplan and Norton, 2004). Four questions to ask related to these perspectives are: 1) To achieve our vision, how should we appear to our customers?, 2) To satisfy our customers, which operational processes must we excel at?, 3) How will we sustain our ability to change and improve?, and 4) To financially sustain our mission, what must we focus on?

Step Three: Implement the Action Plan
✔ Identify time frames.

✔ Establish your career center as an entity.
  • Recruit and hire staff.
  • Evaluate materials.
  • Develop a plan for organizing and maintaining resources.
  • Choose a permanent location.
  • Select a design and layout for the center.
  • Locate necessary equipment.
  • Consider how to respond to new and emerging technology.
  • Market to appropriate constituencies.

✔ Enlist supporters/partners to increase visibility or collaborate in delivering services (with help from the advisory group).

✔ Communicate with key elements of your public.

✔ Practice continuous planning and improvement.
- Engage in continuous discussion to develop or review mission, purpose, and roles.
- Create a plan for integrating/infusing evaluation findings into practice.

✔ Ask regularly: "What are the concerns/challenges/needs of the population we serve?" This, of course, returns you to Step One.

✔ Critical to the success in planning is not seeing the process as stagnate. The continuous planning and improvement processes help career centers stay current, in touch with their users, and watching the horizon for needed action that can be handled proactively.

SUMMARY

Many people in today's workforce got into their current positions through hard work, low to moderate levels of planning, and happenstance. There is little doubt that to succeed in today's workforce, a more thoughtful and organized approach can add to one's success.

It is important to carefully examine the conceptual foundation that guides the development of the career center, and to recognize (and then publicize) the role of the center in the career development processes of individuals. Further, identifying individual needs and then providing developmentally appropriate support, services, and activities is a cornerstone of effective practice.

While a magic formula for creating a career center would be ideal, no such formula exists. Success results from your capacity to take these suggestions and recommendations, translate them into useful processes and systems that are sensitive to the demands within your environment, and combine them with your unique community resources to meet the needs of your audience.

CHAPTER 14

What Does the Future Hold?

By Carl McDaniels, Ph.D.
and updated by Brian M. Montalvo, Ed.S.

In the future, it may be convenient to point to a computer and say: "That is our career center! Everything you need is in there." But what a mistake that would be! Career centers for the future need a far more thoughtful and comprehensive approach than just that. They should be multidimensional to accommodate their users' many different learning styles. They should reflect the modern world of work and the modern approach to preparing for it and living in it.

This chapter suggests some, but not necessarily all, of the signposts that will guide career centers in the future. These are meant to be suggestions for most settings and will probably trigger other ideas as local needs dictate. The one point that all career centers need to consider, now as well as in the future, is the need to be user-friendly. This is implied in the 10 signposts below as well as in the 11 previous chapters. After the very best career center is planned and developed, it is only effective if people use it to the fullest possible extent. There has to be a major ongoing effort to make centers attractive, inviting, comfortable, bright, accessible, relevant, and most important, helpful, to a variety of users.

TEN SIGNPOSTS FOR CAREER CENTERS OF THE FUTURE

Signpost 1: Firsthand Experience in the Best Source of Career Information

The best source of career information has always been personal experience. It may now be called experiential learning or hands-on learning, but it still means getting out and learning about education and employment firsthand. For example, it has always been better to visit a college for a few days when classes are in session than read about it in a brochure. It is infinitely better to see, feel, and smell the campus than to take a virtual tour on its Web site. Likewise, the best way to judge continuing education efforts is to visit a class instead of reading a course description. It's not always possible to arrange firsthand experiences, but it is always best to make the effort. A key element in an effective and comprehensive career center for the future is full-scale arrangements for direct versus indirect experience; this is where the center's connections to the local community pay off.

Career centers can arrange or direct a user toward

- part-time work opportunities, both long- and short-term;
- summer employment, possibly as replacements for vacationing workers;
- volunteer opportunities in local, state, or national programs;
- service-learning experiences;
- occupational and educational information interviewing;
- job shadowing experiences;
- cooperative work-study opportunities;
- internships;
- ongoing relationships with occupational mentors and role models;
- visits to institutions of higher learning; and
- summer camp experience on college campuses.

Developing those firsthand experiences and linking to the community also builds the awareness of the center itself, which is often a vital lifeline for career center existence.

A good example of the potential "costs" to a lack of awareness of services can be found in career centers located on college campuses. This can be detrimental because "a lack of familiarity with the benefits provided to the college or university by the career center can make the career center a target for budget freezes and reductions" (Hammond 2001, p. 188). According to Davidson, Heppner, and Johnston (2001) "staff members will be expected to have skills and competencies that are far more extensive that ever before, far from being simply providers of information, centers must reconsider how, why, where, and when they are reaching their clientele" (p.150). Reardon, Sampson, and Lenz (2000) also suggest that given the emerging roles, relationships, and context for career service delivery, there is much speculation that career assessments will increasingly focus on determining readiness for career problem solving and decision making. These factors will become crucial as the core value of career centers lies in its two-fold mission of: (1) assisting students in making effective decisions about their major and career; and (2) assisting students in obtaining appropriate employment and experiential learning to enhance their movement toward their career goal (Hammond 2001). While this example relates to college career centers, the transferability to career centers in most environments is clear.

Signpost 2: Multimedia Approach

Just as in today's libraries, tomorrow's career centers must accommodate a variety of learning styles. Some users who are not computer literate may feel more comfortable taking home a magazine or newspaper featuring vocational information. Others may choose to watch a video rather than to read a book, or they may want to call a career information hotline to speak directly to a professional. The point is simple and obvious: the career center that takes a one-dimensional approach to disseminating information will serve only a very limited number and narrow band of clients. That may be acceptable in a facility serving only college graduates who are all highly literate and computer literate as well. More often, however, career centers must deal with users who have varying reading levels and technological competence. To ensure a true multimedia approach, career centers should aim for the following kinds of resources:

- Print materials such as occupational and educational newspapers (general and specialized), magazines, brochures, books, pamphlets, reprints, monographs, and briefs
- Large visuals including posters and pictures on all aspects of users' career development, such as financial aid, apprenticeships, state licensed occupations, fastest growing career fields, local training options, and accredited home study programs
- Audio and video tapes on an appropriate range of career topics for the target user groups (CDs, DVDs)
- Access to appropriate computer software and Internet access to at least one local, state, regional, or national career information delivery system (CIDS)
- Career information telephone hotlines, ideally linked to another career center, a CIDS, or similar source

Career center libraries (resource centers) should also consider how they are going to effectively manage the extensive amount of data and resources that are readily available. The role that a career resource library plays in a career center depends on the nature of the center, and thus may vary greatly from center to center (Sampson, Peterson, Reardon, and Lenz 2004). Career centers in the future will benefit from compartmentalizing their resources using theory. For example, smaller career center libraries can organize their resources in terms of Holland's RIASEC theory. This will involve grouping resources by the six distinctive Holland types. All resources dealing with Holland's *social* type (teaching, counseling, etc.) could be grouped together and so forth. Cognitive information processing theory can also assist career center libraries in organizing their resources into different domains, "integrating the career information search with the development of self-knowledge, occupational knowledge, decision making skills, and metacognitions" (Sampson et al. 2004, p. 253). Historically career center libraries have been managed by counselors and/or paraprofessionals. With the increasing demand for providing relevant up-to-date information through various multimedia resources, career centers of the future may want to partner-up or seek the assistance of professionally trained librarians who can systematically organize the resources.

Signpost 3: Serving Diverse Users, Especially Women, Minorities, and Persons with Disabling Conditions of All Age Levels

Obviously, other specific groups such as veterans, retirees, and those who speak English as a second language could also be highlighted here. The point is that the increasing diversity of users must be fully accommodated in future career centers. Here are the three general suggestions:

1. Provide access to mentors and role models from various groups who can personally relate to the users' problems and concerns. In recent pre-employment activities with persons moving from welfare-to-work, two things made the greatest impact: (a) Role models formerly on welfare but now successful wage-earners, family members, and lifelong learners; and (b) Mentors who were there on a continuing basis for comfort, understanding, and encouragement.
2. Provide print materials, Web sites and software that speak to diverse groups. Make a special effort to show that the modern world of work is open to all.
3. Take advantage of the latest technology to assist users with special needs. Ready access to TDD and TYY phone connections are as necessary as books in Braille and other

special assistive devices. Specialized software and Web sites are increasingly becoming available for the diverse groups.

Signpost 4: The Changing Workplace: Flextime, Flexplace, Flexpay, Job Sharing, Part Time, Contingency Work, and Temporary Work

Full-time, long-term employment with a single company is no longer as common as it once was, and future career centers will need to deal with that. People are often astonished to learn that Manpower (http://www.manpower.com)—the temporary hiring firm—employs more people than any other company in the United States. This firm, along with Kelly Services (http://www. kellyservices.com), and hundreds of other temping firms around the country, should be presented as real options for adults seeking less than regular full-time employment. Job sharing and part-time jobs also deserve consideration.

Likewise, information about flexible working arrangements needs to be a part of career centers in the future. Such arrangements may be made at the convenience of the employee, the employer, or both. Flextime may involve working a shift, say 9:00 A.M. to 3:00 P.M., that allows a parent to be at home whenever school-age children are there. Flexplace may provide work-at-home (or telecommuting) options. In any case, there are more and more options beyond the traditional workweek that career center users may want to explore for a variety of family, educational, personal, or financial reasons.

Signpost 5: Small Business Opportunities

Many of the fastest growing employment opportunities across the United States are in small business. Most often defined as employers with fewer than 500 employees, small businesses are more likely to have only 25 to 100 employees. For the most part, they are firms less than 25 years old, often involved in health care technology, or service-related fields. Beyond the famous success stories of Micro-soft, Dell computers, and Google, there are hundreds of successful small businesses in almost every career field, from publishing to landscaping. Career centers need to feature opportunities in small businesses just as much as large corporations or multinational firms.

One major aspect of small business that career centers can easily feature is that of franchises. Many of the small employers in most communities are franchise operations, such as

- Fast food: Burger King, Subway, McDonald's, Wendy's
- Gasoline: Exxon, Chevron, Shell, Mobile
- Auto dealers: Chrysler, Ford, GM, Honda, Subaru
- Motels: Comfort Inn, Hampton Inn, Holiday Inn, Days Inn
- Pizza: Papa John's, Domino's, Pizza Hut
- Miscellaneous: Enterprise Rent-a-Car, Jiffy Lube, Mail Boxes, Etc.

To properly feature small business opportunities, it is important to have the latest books, software, and Web sites (e.g. http://www.inc.com/, http://www.franchise.org/), and other information on this important area of future employment. A great resource is the U.S. Small Business Administration (formerly known as the Small Business Associations), which can be reached by phone at (800) U-ASK-SBA (800-827-5722) or TTY: (704) 344-6640, by e-mail at answerdesk@sba.gov, or on the Web at http://www.sba.gov.

Signpost 6: Entrepreneurship

One of the dominant forces in the economy of the next century (and the source of much of its job growth) will be entrepreneurship. This usually involves innovative ideas characterized by uncertainty and risk, complementary managerial competencies, and creative opportunism. These factors distinguish entrepreneurship from other small business or work-at-home opportunities. Bringing this concept to career center users may mean locating examples of successful entrepreneurs as well as illustrations of how products and services can be targeted toward unfulfilled niche markets, such as ones filled by Michael Dell with Dell Computers and Debbie Field with Mrs. Field's Cookies. A further reason to feature entrepreneurship in career centers is the great promise this area offers for women, minorities, and people with disabling conditions. Community contacts and various multimedia resources including *Black Enterprise* (http://www.blackenterprise.com) and *Entrepreneur* (http://www.entrepreneur.com), can help career centers of the future emphasize this exciting career option.

Signpost 7: Work-at-Home Opportunities

Although no exact figures are available, a population survey in 1997 revealed 3.6 million (3.3 percent) of all wage and salary workers received pay for work done at home (Marian 2000). This is a formidable number and a good reason for including information about this important area of work in the career center of the future. Work-at-home simply refers to people who work out of their apartments, houses, farms, etc. Some people who work at home are self-employed. There are four general categories of work-at-home self-employment:

1. Traditional: accountant, cosmetologist, insurance salesperson, photographer, graphic designer
2. Direct Sales: Amway, Avon, Fuller Brush, Mary Kay, Tupperware
3. Craft: calligrapher, leather-worker, potter, quilter
4. Miscellaneous: bed and breakfast, catering, cleaning, pet grooming, consulting, and Web site development

Other people who work at home are employed by outside firms, doing work such as sales, writing, or data entry. Hewlett Packard, the technology company that produces computers, televisions, and other products, runs most of its technical support services with employees working from home. Some people combine this kind of work with self-employment.

With such large numbers of people involved in work-at-home and every indication that their numbers will continue to grow, career centers must begin to present information on this as a career option. Resources in this area are somewhat difficult to find, but there are some good small newsletters, Web sites, and magazines such as *Working Solo* (http://www.workingsolo.com/newsletter/newslettersignup.html), *Home Business Magazine* (http://www.homebusinessmag.com), and a variety of books. Again, the career center's connections to the local community can really pay off by connecting its clients with mentors and role models from the work-at-home sector.

Signpost 8: Serving Older Adults

Demographics strongly suggest that the career center of the future will need to serve older adults, the most rapidly growing segment of the American population. Right now, roughly one-third of the population is 50 years of age or older and, because of the aging of the baby boom generation, that percentage is growing faster than any other age group. For the most part, this group is mobile and can afford many of the educational opportunities now open to them on a full- or part-time basis. For many, this means the chance to complete a degree begun years ago or to pursue an interest in art, drama, landscaping, or computers that was not practical or even available when they were last in school. There are now many opportunities open only to people over 55 years of age, such as Elder-hostels. Elderhostel sponsors one- to three-week learning programs across the United States, Canada, Europe, and more than 70 foreign countries; more information is available at 11 Avenue de Lafayette, Boston, MA 02111 or on their Web site at http://www.elderhostel.org. They can also be reached Toll-Free at (800) 454-5768.

In addition to educational information for older adults, occupational information related to signposts 5, 6, and 7 above is very important. For the older adult who wants to work at home, this may be the perfect time to try to turn a hobby into a lucrative business. Speaking of hobbies, since the older population is living longer and staying healthier, the career center that serves this population is advised to provide up-to-date information on leisure activities as well. The interaction between leisure and work is much more apparent to older adults than to younger people, particularly when the definition of leisure includes physical, social, intellectual, volunteer, and creative activities.

Signpost 9: Serving Low-Income Persons, Unemployed Persons, and those Affected by Natural Disasters or Other Casastrophes

One of the biggest challenges of the future from a career development standpoint is how to improve career center services for low-income and unemployed clients. The most obvious illustration of this was the nationwide effort called *welfare-to-work* (the Welfare-to-Work program officially ended on September 30, 2004). According to the U.S. Department of Health and Human Services, welfare reform helped move 4.7 million Americans from welfare dependency to self-sufficiency within three years of enactment, and the number of welfare caseloads has declined by 54 percent since 1996 (for more information on welfare reform go to http://www.acf.hhs. gov/acf_services.html). This group, as well as the people affected by events such as Hurricane Katrina or the 9/11 terrorist attacks, needs career center services working during a time of crisis. For many of these workers the way up (either for the first time or again) may be through more training and education. This may, in fact, prove the largest and most significant role a career center might play in the next 10 to 20 years as welfare reform and relief programs for displaced workers send increasing numbers of people to career centers for help. Similar groups caught up in a personal crisis and in search of career services will include those workers displaced by downsizing, mergers, outsourcing, or closures who have some skills but need additional training and guidance to re-enter the workforce.

Across the nation the tragic events of natural disasters and the attacks of 9/11 have led people to reflect on their current occupations and determine whether or not they are satisfied with their current choice. More and more people will seek out occupations that fit their interests, values, and needs. Bolles (2005) stresses the importance of helping people find their "mission." Assisting people search/discover their "missions" or helping them realign their occupational beliefs with their spiritual beliefs will be a challenge for career centers to face. Over the past couple of years there has been much written about the connection between a chosen occupation with spiritual beliefs (Adams and Csiernik 2002; Bloch 2004; Cervantes and Parha 2005; Colozzi and Colozzi 2000; Garcia-Zamor 2003). Duffy (2006, p. 58) states that "empirical explorations of the extent and the nature of the spirituality, religiousness, and career development relationship have just begun." Career centers of the future will need to have readily available resources on this topic as well as have counselors on the staff who are aware of the role who spirituality can play on career decision.

Special consideration must be given to the resources needed by the growing user group of unemployed, underemployed, displaced, or low-income persons. Reading levels, attractiveness, and accessibility are especially important to these groups. The creation of "mini-career centers" in libraries, community centers, and welfare offices may be needed as well as the creation of "mobile career centers" that can go on location whenever the need arises. More personal assistance may be necessary for people who have been out of work, disconnected from education for many years, and/or recently experienced a traumatic event. The availability of mentors, role models, support staff, and paraprofessionals (e.g., career development facilitators) through career centers may be the most important resource of all. The one-stop career centers (established under the Workforce Investment Act, 1998) are coordinated by the Department of Labor's Employment and Training Administration (ETA). ETA's Web site provides a clickable map of One-Stop Center's Web sites for each state. It also provides a list of state, regional, and local center contacts. Locate a center by calling ETA's toll-free help line at (877) US-2JOBS. The U.S. Department of Labor's ETA program will serve some members of this large user group, but career centers in every community will have to be prepared to serve them as well.

It also worth noting that with every passing year career centers as a whole are becoming an integral part of national labor market policies. Herr (2003, p. 8) discussed three specific areas where this will become evident: "(a) the prevention or the reduction of long-term unemployment, the development of an effective workforce, and the matching of workers and employers; (b) the adjustment by employed workers to rapidly changing labor market conditions, including the pervasive use of advanced technology in the workplace; (c) the provision of assistance to persons considered marginally employable because of poor skills, functional disabilities, social problems, or work requirements with which they cannot cope without significant help."

Signpost 10: Self-Directed Assessment
Frank Parsons, the "father of vocational guidance," emphasized in his 1909 book, *Choosing a Vocation,* three broad factors in vocational choice: understand yourself, understand the world of work, and engage in true reasoning based on these two groups of facts. The first part of this process has often been misunderstood or overlooked in favor of the "test 'em and tell 'em" method: give a test (also known as an assessment) and it will reveal what persons are like and what they should be. In the future, there should be renewed consideration of Parson's (and more recently Richard Bolles) notion of self-discovery and self-understanding by way of self-directed assessment. Such a process would ideally include one or more of the firsthand experiences mentioned at the first signpost in this chapter, which give clients an idea of their strengths and weaknesses as well as their likes and dislikes.

Self-directed assessment has attracted considerable attention, which can be seen in the growing number of self-assessment instruments on the market. Some are improved interest inventories; others help make a connection between leisure interests in portfolio development. Future career centers will have the tools and organizational capabilities they need to make self-directed assessment a featured service.

BECOMING MORE COMPREHENSIVE

One additional future trend, reflected in what is happening in the following example from career centers in higher education settings, may be the move toward becoming more comprehensive in the nature and scope of services. The four continuua summarized below (from Vernick, Garis, and Reardon 2000) provide a glimpse into that trend:

1. The degree to which career centers hold missions for providing career development services through career advising, counseling, assessment, and information. Career centers that are involved in all facets of career development services fall to the far right of this continuum. The ones that fall to the left are the ones that may provide assistance with employability skills but do not offer programs for academic/career choice or career indecision.

2. The degree to which the career center provides experiential career education services (e.g., externships, internships, and cooperative education) as part of their mission. Career centers that shoulder the full responsibility for experiential education programs fall to the far right of this continuum. At the other end are universities that have experiential programs through their academic units rather than the career center. More commonly one finds experiential programs that are shared by academic units and the career center, the middle of this continuum.

3. The degree to which the career center has placement, or employer relations services decentralized to centralized. Career centers that have employer relationships throughout different placement offices in academic units reside at the far left of this continuum. Career centers that have employer relationships centralized in the career center are at the other end of this continuum.

4. The degree to which the career center is funded by the institution can also be plotted on a continuum. Career centers that are not funded by the institution and instead have to rely on generating operating budget through fund-raising fall on the far left of the continuum. University career centers that rely solely of the institution for funding fall at the other end. Most successful comprehensive career centers receive funding from the institution as well as generate funds through various activities.

Career services that fall on the right side of the four continuua summarized above would generally be considered to be more comprehensive career centers. These comprehensive career centers would typically offer these core programs: (1) career advising and intake, (2) individual and group counseling, (3) assessment and computer-assisted guidance, (4) career information, career planning classes for credit, (5) career education outreach, (6) experiential education, (7) career expositions, (8) on-campus recruiting, and (9) job listing and resume referral services (Vernick et al. 2000).

FINALLY, NEVER BE SATISFIED

Two studies still apply today. The first is the American Council on Education's *Too Little Knowledge is a Dangerous Thing: What the Public Thinks and Knows about Paying for College*. This study found that most adults have no clue as to how much a college education costs, where students can find financial aid, and just how much aid is available. The authors commented that "the public continues to grossly overestimate the price of going to college and many believe that it is unaffordable for a majority of families." Specifically, the study found that parents overestimated the cost of tuition by three times the accurate amount! The second study, by ACT, revealed that 42 percent of high school seniors who took the ACT exam said they needed more assistance with educational and occupational planning, and very small percentages were selecting majors in computer and information science or computer engineering, the occupations with the highest projected rate of growth over the next decade. Clearly, these two studies demonstrate that today's college students and their parents are badly in need of accurate, up-to-date, timely, and usable career information, the kind that should be readily available and properly managed in every career center.

A key point in all of the signposts of trends affecting career centers in the future is the idea that it should always be a work-in-progress. Career centers should always be thought of as being under construction and never completed, never good enough. There must always be new ideas and methods under consideration, existing resources under review. It has been suggested that a career center keep nothing over five years old except perhaps a section of "golden-oldies" or time-honored resources offering enduring ideas.

And, as has been noted throughout this book, the career center for the future must engage in constant evaluation as part of never being satisfied. This means that everyone who uses the center must have input in its services and future direction, along with special focus groups and advisory boards. The staff should be constantly searching for better ways to provide assistance through personal service and expanded resources. There are always more convenient hours and more accessible floor plans for the center to examine. There is always new technology to consider and evaluate. There are always new and better local resources waiting to be incorporated into the career center's services. There are always new things for the staff to learn, workshops and conferences to attend, and professional credentials to pursue. Indeed, career centers of the future may find challenges in meeting new accreditation standards that will program self-study and independent, outside review. Ultimately, future career centers, like those of the past and present, will need to fit varied types of information and resources together into a delivery system that is constantly under review and improvement for the optimum career development of each user.

BIBLIOGRAPHY

Adams, D. W., and R. Csiernik. Seeking the lost spirit: Understanding spirituality and restoring it to the workplace. *Employee Assistance Quarterly* 17 (2002): 31-44.

Amundson, N. E. "Supporting Clients through a Change in Perspective." *Journal of Employment Counseling* 33 (1996): 155-162.

Bingham, R. P., and C. Ward. "Career Counseling with Ethnic Minority Women." In *Career Counseling With Women,* edited by W. Walsh and S. H. Osipow (pp. 165–195). Hillsdale, N.J.: Erlbaum, 1994.

Bloch, D. P. "Spirituality, complexity, and career counseling." *Professional School Counseling* 7 (2004): 343-350.

Bluestein, D. L. *The Psychology of Working.* Mahwah, N.J.: Lawrence Erlbaum, 2006.

Boettger, Marsha. "The Evolution of a Corporate Career Center." *Career Planning and Adult Development* 16, no. 2 (2000): 46–50.

Bolles, R. N. *How to Find Your Mission in Life.* Berkeley, Calif: Ten Speed Press, 2005.

Bolles, R. N. *What Color Is Your Parachute?* Berkeley, Calif.: Ten Speed, 2000.

Bosworth, K. and Walz, G. R. *Promoting Student Resiliency.* Alexandria, Va.: American Counseling Association Foundation, 2005.

Bridges, W. *Job Shift.* New York: Addison-Wesley, 1994.

Bureau of Labor Statistics. *News: United States Department of Labor (USDL Publication No. 02-497).* Washington, D.C.: United States Government Printing Office, 2002.

Byars-Winston, A. M. and N. A. Fouad. "Metacognition and Multicultural Competence: Expanding the Culturally Appropriate Career Counseling Model." *Career Development Quarterly* 54 (2006).

Cervantes, J. M. and T.A. Parham. "Toward a meaningful spirituality for people of color: Lessons for the counseling practitioner." *Cultural Diversity & Ethic Minority Psychology* 11 (2005): 69-81.

Colozzi, E. A., and L.C. Colozzi. "College students' callings and careers: An integrated values-oriented perspective." In D.A. Luzzo (Ed.), *Career Counseling of College Students: An Empirical Guide to Strate-*

gies that Work (pp. 63-91). Washington, DC: American Psychological Association, 2000.

Davidson, M. M., M. J. Heppner, and J. A. Johnston. "Transforming career centers for the new millennium." *Journal of Career Development* 27, no. 3 (2001): 149-151.

Evans, K. M., and J. C. Rotter, "Multicultural Family Approaches to Career Counseling." *The Family Journal* 8 (2000): 67-71.

Fouad, N. A., and R. Bingham. "Career Counseling with Racial/Ethnic Minorities." In *Handbook of Vocational Psychology*, edited by W. B. Walsh and S. H. Opinow (pp. 331-366). Hillsdale, N.J.: Erlbaum, 1995.

Frasier, James R. Preface to *First Motorola Worldwide Learning, Training and Education Research Conference*, edited by James R. Frasier. Schaumburg, Ill.: Motorola University Press, 1995.

Frodsham, Joe, and Bill Gargiulo. *Make it Work: Navigate Your Career without Leaving Your Organization*. Mountain View, Calif.: Davies-Black Publishing, 2005.

Fulmer, Robert M. "Choose Tomorrow's Leaders Today, Succession Planning Grooms Firms for Success." *Graziadio Business Report, Journal of Contemporary Business Practice*. Available online. http://gbr.pepperdine.edu/021/succession.html. Retrieved on April 26, 2007.

Garica-Zamor, J. C. "Workplace Spirituality and Organizational Performance." *Public Administration Review* 63 (2003): 355-363.

Gelatt, H. B. *Creative Decision Making: Using Positive Uncertainty*. Los Altos, Calif.: Crisp, 1991.

Goodman, J., Schlossberg, N. K., and Anderson, M. L. *Counseling Adults in Transition*, 3rd ed., New York: Springer, 2006.

Gilley, J. and S. Eggland. *Principles of Human Resource Development*. New York: Addison-Wesley, 1997.

Goodman, J., and N. Savage. "Responding to a Community Need: Oakland University's Adult Career Counseling Center." *The Career Development Quarterly* 48 (1999): 19-30.

Hammond, M. S. "Career Centers and Needs Assessments: Getting the Information You Need to Increase Your Success." *Journal of Career Development* 27, no. 3 (2001); 187-197.

Hansen, L. S. "Integrative Life Planning (ILP): A Holistic Theory for Career Counseling with Adults." In *Adult Career Development: Con-*

cepts, Issues, and Practices, edited by S. Niles. Tulsa, Okla.: National Career Development Association, 2002.

Heady, Thomas S. "The Right Prescription: The Eli Lilly & Company Career Center." *Career Planning and Adult Development* 16, no. 2 (2000): 51–55.

Herr, E. L., Cramer, S. H., and Niles, S. G. *Career Guidance and Counseling through the Lifespan,* 6th ed. Boston: Pearson, 2004.

Herr, E. L. "The Future of Career Counseling as an Instrument of Public Policy: Career Counseling in the Next Decade." *Career Development Quarterly* 52, no. 1 (2003): 8-10.

Kaye, Beverly. *Up Is Not the Only Way; A Guide to Developing Workforce Talent.* Palo Alto, Calif.: Davies-Black Publishing, 1997.

Knowdell, Richard L. *Building A Career Development Program.* Palo Alto, Calif.: Davies-Black Publishing, 1996.

Knowdell, Richard L., Elizabeth Brandstead, and Milan Moravec. *From Downsizing to Recovery: Strategic Transition Options for Organizations and Individuals.* Palo Alto, Calif.: Davies-Black Publishing, 1996.

Mariani, M. "Telecommuters." *Occupational Outlook Quarterly,* 44, no.3 (2000): 10-17. In Reardon R. C., Lenz, J. G., Sampson J. P., and Peterson G. W. *Career Development and Planning: A Comprehensive Approach,* 2nd ed. (p. 136.) Mason, OH: Thomson, 2006.

Miller, C. Hall, S. Kelemen, L., and Klinck, K. *Adult Career Counseling Center: Twenty-Third Annual Report.* Rochester, Minn.: Oakland, University, 2006.

Niles, S. G., and Harris-Bowlsbey, J. *Career Development Interventions in the Twenty-first Century.* Upper Saddle River, N.J.: Merrill Prentice Hall, 2002.

Niles, S. G., E. L. Herr, and P. J. Hartung. "Adult Career Concerns in Contemporary Society." In *Adult Career Development: Concepts, Issues, and Practices,* edited by S. Niles. Tulsa, Okla.: National Career Development Association, 2002.

Patch, Ken. "An Historical Overview of Corporate Career Centers." *Career Planning and Adult Development* 16, no. 2 (2000): 7–12.

Patch, Ken. "Future Vision: A Look into the Twenty-First Century." *Career Planning and Adult Development* 16, no. 2 (2000): 97–103.

Patch, Ken. "A Systems Thinking Approach to Career Development." In *First Motorola Worldwide Learning, Training and Education Research Conference.* Schaumburg, Ill.: Motorola University Press, 1995.

Peterson, L. *Starting Out, Starting Over.* Palo Alto, Calif.: Davies-Black, 1995.

Reardon, R., J. Lenz, J. Sampson, and Peterson, G. *Career Development and Planning: A Comprehensive Approach.* Mason, OH: Brooks/Cole, Thompson Learning, 2000.

Reardon, R., J. Lenz, J. Sampson, and Peterson, G. "Career Assessment in a Time of Changing Roles, Relationships, and Contexts." *Journal of Career Assessment* 8, no. 4 (2000): 351-359.

Rheault, Magali. "Happy Birthday Boomers." *Kiplinger.Com* May 31, 2006, p. 1. Available online. http://www.kiplinger.com/features/archives/2006/05/boomers.html Retrieved on April 26, 2007.

Rifkin, J. *The End of Work.* New York: Putnam, 1995.

Rouda, Robert H. and Mitchell E. Kusy, Jr. "Career Development, Personal Career Management and Planning; Development of Human Resources — Part 4." *Tappi Journal.* Available online. http://alumnus.caltech.edu/~rouda/T4_CD.html Retrieved on April 26, 2007.

Sampson J. P. Jr., G. W. Peterson, R. C. Reardon, and G. J. Lenz. *Career Counseling and Services: A Cognitive Information Processing Approach.* Belmont, Calif: Brooks/Cole, 2004.

Savickas, M. "The Spirit in Career Counseling: Fostering Self-Completion through Work." In *Connections Between Spirit and Work in Career Development: New Approaches and Practical Perspectives,* edited by D. P. Block and L. J. Richmond. Palo Alto, Calif.: Davies-Black, 1997.

Schlossberg, N. K. *Retire Smart, Retire Happy: Finding Your True Path in Life.* Washington, D.C.: American Psychological Association, 2004.

Schlossberg, N. K. "A Model for Analyzing Human Adaptation to Transition." *The Counseling Psychologist* 9 (1981): 2-18.

Toossi, M. "The Century of Change: The U.S. Labor Force, 1950–2050." *Monthly Labor Review* 125 (2002): 15-28.

Tyson, L. E. and P. B. Pederson. "What My Daughter Does Is None of Your Business!" *Critical Incidents in School Counseling,* edited by L. E. Tyson and P.B. Pederson (pp. 21-232). Alexandria, Va.: American Counseling Association, 2000.

Vernick, S., J. Garis, and R. Reardon. "Integrating Service, Teaching, and Research in A Comprehensive University Career Center." *Career Planning & Adult Development Journal* 16 (2000): 7-24.

Watts, A.G. "Career Development and Public Policy." *Educational and Vocational Guidance Bulletin*, 64 (2000): 9-21.

Zunker, Vernon G. *Career Counseling: Applied Concepts of Life Planning.* Pacific Grove, Calif.: Brooks/Cole, 2002.

CONTRIBUTORS

Judith Ettinger, Ph.D. is a Senior staff member at the Center on Education and Work at the University of Wisconsin—Madison. She has been working in the field of career development for the past 30 years. She is also a lecturer in the Counseling Psychology Department at the University of Wisconsin. In that capacity she teaches courses on Facilitating Career Development. Judith also teaches an online course on career assessments at UCLA. In addition, she is a trainer for the National Institute of Corrections and one of the co-authors of the National Career Development Guidelines.

Pat Fessenden, Ph.D. is Assistant Dean Emerita of Adult and Student Services at the University of Wisconsin—Madison. She was the first person to head a unit blending educational and career counseling services for community adults with the admission office for non-degree students in 1996. She has worked over thirty years in student services at Wisconsin, in addition to service at Marquette, and Ohio State University, where she earned her Ph.D. in 1976. Fessenden has served in leadership positions on the Wisconsin College Personnel Association, National Association of Academic Administrators, UW's Student Personnel Association, Academic Staff Executive Committee, and Associate Administrative Council.

Jane Finkle, M.S., NCC is a Career Counselor at Bryn Mawr College and Co Founder of Career Visions in Philadelphia has over 20 years experience helping individuals with career assessment and planning, job search strategies and workplace adjustment. She advises Internet users nationwide for *US News and World Report's* online Education and Career Forum and teaches a Career Evaluation Course at the University of Pennsylvania. Jane is President of the Philadelphia Chapter of the Association of Career Management Professionals-International and is a member of the National Career Development Association. She has an M.S. in Counseling from the University of Rochester, and is a National Certified Counselor (NCC).

212

Jane Goodman, Ph.D., recently retired from her position as Professor, Counseling at Oakland University in Rochester, Michigan. Dr. Goodman was the 2001-2002 president of the American Counseling Association and is a past president of the National Career Development Association and the 2006 winner of NCDA's Eminent Career Award. She is the author of many articles and book chapters, primarily in the area of transitions and career development, including the third edition of *Counseling Adults in Transition* (with Nancy Schlossberg and Mary Anderson) and the *NCDA Case Book* (with Skip Niles and Mark Pope). She is the mother or stepmother of seven and has eight grandchildren on whom she dotes.

Carl McDaniels, Ph.D., is a noted career expert who has served as a counselor and educator for more than 50 years. He has served as president of the Virginia Career Development Association and the National Career Development Association.

Brian Montalvo, Ed. S. is currently the Assistant Director of Florida Atlantic University's Career Development Center (Boca Raton Campus). His primary responsibilities include, but are not limited to, managing the Career Development Center's career counseling and assessment programs. Brian is a Nationally Certified Counselor and a Florida State Seminole three-times-over, receiving his B.S. (psychology), M.S. (counseling and human systems), and his Ed.S. (counseling and human systems) all from Florida State University. Brian is also always thankful to Dr. Robert C. Reardon for his continual guidance and encouragement.

Ken Patch, Ph.D., uniquely combined education, counseling and business in a variety of settings; Corporate Director, Career Management for Motorola, provided counseling for employees and leadership coaching for across all levels including organizational VPs and Presidents. Designed and developed the Masters in Education, School Counseling for University of Phoenix, taught in that program as well as the MC Counseling program for UOP; designed Counseling Masters for Ottawa University; initiated and developed Hopi Reservation branch campus of the newly established Northland Pioneer College. Native American Counselor for Phoenix College; as Director, developed and managed the Phoenix Indian High School Pupil Personnel Services program as pilot for Bureau of Indian Affairs, provided counseling grades 7-12 (awarded Arizona APGA "Outstanding Program." Active in professional associations over the past 30 years (AzCA, ACDA, ASTD, HOE, Adult Ed, NCDA (national board) and others.

Sybil Pressprich, M.Ed., is a Senior Counselor in the Adult and Student Services Center at the University of Wisconsin—Madison where she provides individual career and educational counseling for adults facing career transitions. She facilitates a weekly job search support group and develops and delivers career development workshops to community members. In addition, she provides on site career services and workshops to local area employers. She is active in the Wisconsin Career Development Association and speaks to groups on career development topics.

Becky Ryan, M.S., is the Associate Director with the Cross-College Advising Service. As a veteran CCAS staff member, she headed the development of the career exploration center at CCAS. She has worked as an independent outplacement career counselor and Family Life consultant. She has served in numerous leadership roles including serving as the National Academic Advising Association Regional chair, President of the Wisconsin Academic Advising Association (WACADA), President of the Madison Academic Staff Association, and Chair of the L&S Personnel Policies and Procedures Committee (PDRC). She frequently presents in the area of career and academic advising, and advisor training and development.

Donald A. Schutt Jr., Ph.D., NCC is the Director of Human Resource Development in the Office of Human Resources at the University of Wisconsin-Madison where he manages the development and delivery of centralized professional and career development workshops for over 18,000 employees. Previously, he worked as a career development specialist at the Center on Education and Work in the School of Education at UW-Madison. He has presented over 300 workshops and authored several publications. Don is a Licensed Professional Counselor in the state of Wisconsin as well as a National Certified Counselor and a Master Career Development Professional. His educational background includes a Ph.D. and M.A. in Counselor Education from the University of Iowa, and a B.A. in Journalism and Economics from UW—Madison.

Pat Schwallie-Giddis, Ph.D., Associate Professor at George Washington University and the Program Director in the Department of Counseling/Human and Organizational Studies. She is a national leader in school counseling and a recognized expert in career counseling and career development and serves on the National Career Development Association Board of Directors. Pat received her Ph.D. at Florida State University in Counseling and Human Systems. In October of 1995, she was honored by the university as the "Distinguished Educator of the Year." In 2000, she was honored with the "Distinguished Educator" award from the University of Wisconsin—Platteville where she received her Bachelors and Masters Degrees. She co-authored three books and the most recent is *Counseling Activities for Life Skills and Career Development*, which includes team building, self-management and goal setting.

George Watson, Ed.D., P.M.P. serves as an Internal Consultant in the Office of Quality Improvement at the University of Wisconsin—Madison. He provides consulting services in process improvement, strategic planning, and project management. He is also an adjunct faculty and has held a variety of management roles during the past 25 years in the areas of organizational effectiveness, human resources and information technology. He holds a Doctorate Degree in Human Resource Education from Boston University, a Masters Degree in Business Systems from DePaul Graduate School, a Masters Certificate in Project Management from the University of Wisconsin, and is certified as a Project Management Professional.

INDEX